AFC 6327
23.60
B-00

CRACK

by GILDA BERGER

Revised Edition by
Nancy Levitin

Franklin Watts
New York/Chicago/London/Toronto/Sydney
An Impact Book

FRONTIS: BREAKING UP CRACK TO BE SMOKED

Photographs copyright ©: Black Star: pp. 2, 18 (Joe Rodriguez), 53 (Ken Love), 80 (Martin A. Levick), 98 (Tom Sobolik); Wide World Photos: pp. 8, 13, 43, 49, 50, 55, 56, 61, 75, 91; Cleveland Browns: p. 10; Gamma-Liaison: p. 25 (Arnaud Borrel); Sygma: pp. 27, 65, 111 (Allan Tannenbaum); Picture Group: pp. 58 (Steve Starr), 83, 107 (Danford Connoly); Abbas/Magnum Photos: p. 67; USCG: p. 77 (Dave Anderton); P. Almasy/ WHO Photo: p. 94.

Library of Congress Cataloging-in-Publication Data
Berger, Gilda.
Crack / by Gilda Berger. — Rev. ed. / by Nancy Levitin.
p. cm. — (An Impact book.)
Includes bibliographical references and index.
ISBN 0-531-11188-1
1. Crack (Drug)—Juvenile literature. 2. Youth—United States—Drug use—Juvenile literature. [1. Crack (Drug) 2. Cocaine. 3. Drug abuse.] I. Levitin, Nancy. II. Title.
HV5810.B47 1994
362.29′8—dc20 94-23309 CIP AC

Second Edition
Copyright © 1987, 1994 by Gilda Berger
All rights reserved
Printed in the United States of America
6 5 4 3

CONTENTS

CHAPTER 1
Introduction
7

CHAPTER 2
What Is Crack?
15

CHAPTER 3
Users of Crack
24

CHAPTER 4
Dangers of Crack
34

CHAPTER 5
Manufacture and Sale of Crack
47

CHAPTER 6
Cutting Supply
63

CHAPTER 7
Cutting Demand
79

CHAPTER 8
Care and Treatment
100

Glossary
113

Bibliography
120

For Further Reading
123

For Further Information or Help
124

Index
125

INTRODUCTION

It was 6:32 A.M. on Thursday, June 19, 1986. The phone rang at an emergency center near the University of Maryland. The call came from a dormitory room. Hurriedly, the frantic voice on the phone told them that his friend had stopped breathing.

Paramedics rushed to the university. Immediately they began efforts to revive the victim, a twenty-two-year-old male student. But their attempts failed. There was no pulse or heartbeat. They dashed to the ambulance with the young man and sped off to the nearest hospital, where he was pronounced dead on arrival.

The student was Len Bias, the 6-foot 8-inch (2-m), 210-pound (95-kg) all-American star forward of the University of Maryland basketball team. Bias had just been signed up by the Boston Celtics. Until the moment of his death, the young athlete appeared to have fulfilled his lifelong dream of playing professional basketball.

Bias had spent part of the previous day in Boston with officials of the Celtics. He had also signed a contract to endorse a brand of sneakers that reportedly would have brought him $1 million. All this, in addition to the millions of dollars he would be earning with the Celtics.

College basketball star Len Bias signs with the Boston Celtics in June, 1986.

After completing the deal in Boston, Bias went back to the Maryland campus to celebrate with his friends. The festivities, which started in his campus suite sometime after 2:00 A.M., included the drug cocaine. The first reports indicated that it might be the kind of cocaine known as *crack*. Crack is a very pure form of cocaine that is smoked; other forms of cocaine are sniffed or snorted.

A few hours after Bias started smoking the drug in his Maryland campus dorm room a teammate reportedly told him, "Hey, Len, you're hittin' the pipe too hard." A little later, Bias suffered seizures and collapsed.

An autopsy showed that the Maryland basketball star had a concentration of 6.5 milligrams of cocaine per liter in his blood at the time of his death. (A milligram is 1/1,000 of a gram. A gram is 1/28 of an ounce.) When asked how much cocaine Bias had used, Maryland medical examiner Dr. John Smialek said, "I don't think he took a lot of cocaine. This particular concentration might not have killed another individual."

Apparently, though, even this small amount of cocaine had interrupted the electrical activity in Bias's brain, causing his heart to beat irregularly. The irregular heartbeat, said Dr. Smialek, "resulted in the sudden onset of seizures and cardiac arrest." The final report showed that the cause of death was cocaine—nothing but cocaine.

Exactly one week later, friends gave twenty-three-year-old Don Rogers, the Cleveland Browns' star defensive back, a bachelor party at a Sacramento, California, hotel. Rogers was excited about getting married on June 28 to his college sweetheart, Leslie Nelson.

The 6-foot 1-inch (1.8-m), 206-pound (93-kg) Rogers had attended UCLA on an athletic scholarship. He

Don Rogers, then with the Cleveland Browns, another superstar athlete who fell victim to cocaine in 1986

was an all-American selection and averaged more than a hundred tackles a season. "Donald was one of the greatest football players in UCLA history and had his whole life ahead of him," said Terry Donahue, Rogers's UCLA coach.

Shortly after awakening the next morning, the star defensive back complained about "feeling funny." Then he collapsed. He was taken to a hospital, but the doctors could not revive him. He died without regaining consciousness.

The amount of cocaine doctors found in Rogers's blood was 5.2 milligrams per liter. Dr. Joseph Pawlowski, the pathologist who performed the autopsy, said there was no indication that Rogers was a long-term cocaine user. "There was some interference in the respiratory area of the brain," Dr. Pawlowski said. "Cocaine is most suspect."

Friends and family who expected to attend Rogers's wedding prepared for his funeral instead.

THE SITUATION

The tragic cocaine-related deaths of Bias and Rogers made headlines all over the country. They alerted people, as never before, to the widespread use of cocaine and the hazards that crack, the new form of the drug, pose—especially to the young.

The figures show that cocaine-related injuries and deaths have taken a jump in recent years:

In 1981 Americans consumed about 50 tons of cocaine. By 1985 the consumption had risen to 150 tons. By 1991 over 300,000 metric tons of coca was being brought into the United States.

Medical examiners in twenty-five cities listed 185 cocaine-related deaths in 1981, 580 in 1984, and 563 in just the first part of 1985. In 1991, cocaine was mentioned in 320,000 medical examiners' reports—more than any other drug.

Reports from 700 hospital emergency rooms showed that 3,300 men and women came seeking help for bad reactions to cocaine in 1981. By 1985 that number had more than tripled to 10,000. In 1991, 102,727 admissions to metropolitan hospital emergency rooms were cocaine-related.

The actual number of cocaine-related deaths may be even higher, because most such deaths are reported as something else. Dr. Jeffrey Rosecan, director of the Cocaine Abuse Treatment program at Columbia-Presbyterian Medical Center, has said: "It happens every day that people die of cocaine abuse. Any big-city emergency room has deaths around the clock related to cocaine intoxication. But it's called simply 'cardiac arrest—of undertermined origin.' It's only when there is some notoriety involved that the medical examiner is called in to investigate, as was the case with Len Bias."

"IT CAN'T HAPPEN TO ME"

Dr. Rosecan was asked what he thought Len Bias might have been thinking the night he took the drugs. "I can only guess, of course," said Dr. Rosecan, "but he might have been thinking, 'It can't happen to me. I'm too young, I'm too talented, I'm too smart. I'm invulnerable.'"

Terry Long and David Gregg, roommates of Len Bias, said they did not believe that occasional cocaine use could kill someone. When Bias had the seizures, Long was sure that he would recover. Long said: "It never occurred to me that someone might die. You always think something like that would happen to someone else."

Some days after the deaths of Bias and Rogers, reporters asked youths in several inner-city neighborhoods about the athletes' deaths. Would it make them

The funeral of Len Bias on June 23, 1986. The Reverend Jesse Jackson tries to console Bias's distraught brother.

think twice about drugs? The reactions were mixed.

"I think of Len Bias as a person who just had bad luck," said one. "I've been doing coke for years and look at me: I'm here. I'm healthy."

But another replied, "Something like this is too tragic to forget. To get through all that competition—from the streets to high school to college to the pros. That's what everyone here wants to do. And then to die before you play one pro game. No one will ever forget about that. Len Bias's dream was shattered."

One of the teenagers suggested that Bias was just going along with his friends. But another responded, "You can always say no. Bias should've learned that."

"But when you say no they call you a sucker," a younger boy answered.

"If you can't say no to them, they ain't your friends. They just want to bring you down."

Meanwhile, back on the Maryland campus, a student who said she knew Bias had this to say: "Nobody put a gun to his head and made him take the cocaine. If he had to celebrate, we wish he would have done it some other way."

During a moving funeral service at the Memorial Chapel on the University of Maryland campus, Rev. Jesse Jackson said: "Lenny was vulnerable, but all of us are. It takes years to climb a mountain; one slip and we face oblivion. We must make his death the breaking point."

Our society is rampant with crack and cocaine abuse by people of all races, all ages, and all walks of life. Unfortunately, many young people in particular are falling victim to this epidemic. The responsibility for stemming the tide of deaths belongs to all of us. By learning more about this dangerous drug and avoiding its use we can help to turn things around for everyone.

WHAT IS CRACK?

Pete is twenty-one years old and until recently worked as a security guard in a large auto plant. A high school dropout, he began abusing drugs about four years ago. But his real problems began last winter. This is when he was first introduced to crack.

Pete's girlfriend at the time was smoking crack a few times a month. One day she asked Pete to buy her some of the drug. Then, as Pete later recalled, "Out of curiosity I tried it. I felt euphoric and somewhat light-headed. It was quite addictive. Once you started you didn't want to stop."

Before long, Pete had himself a $100-a-day crack habit. There was one day that his craving for the drug was so strong that he spent nearly $1,000 on crack! He had to steal to get more money. A foreman caught him putting some factory tools in his pocket, and he lost his job.

Pete also took cash and jewelry from his parents' house. Then he began to sneak things out of the homes of neighbors and friends. Gradually, people began to suspect Pete of the crimes. They called him a "crackhead" and a "druggie."

The names made Pete very angry. At first, he covered up his guilt with violent temper tantrums. One time he and his father got into a heated argument about some missing silver. Pete ended up by pushing the older man, who then kicked Pete out of the house.

Pete moved in with his girlfriend. He peddled crack and other drugs on the street to pay for his habit. "I was constantly worried about someone trying to kill me," he confessed.

Occasionally Pete bought his crack in a "crack house," a boarded-up building in a slum neighborhood. It was run by four tough guys who carried guns. Pete reports that he felt "jumpy and more paranoid because of the fear of the police coming in and all those people standing around that you don't know."

He described the scene this way: "Soon as you came in, they searched you. Then you proceeded into another room and they searched you again. When you went to purchase, the guy is behind the wall and so you don't even see him. You put your money into a little drawer."

After a few months on crack, Pete began to suffer violent mood swings. One minute he was happy, active, and talkative. The next, he was overcome with sadness, depression, and lethargy. Normally healthy-looking with a good build, he lost a lot of weight and looked tired and worn.

Also, he felt very lonely. Family members and friends avoided him. His girlfriend wanted nothing more to do with him. "I was wearing out my welcome wherever I went," he explained.

One night, as Pete was wandering the streets, he came upon a street-front drug treatment center. He went in. They offered him a meal and let him talk out his troubles. With their help, Pete is trying to stop smoking crack. But he is having a very hard time giving up his habit.

A NEW MENACE

"Crack" is the street name for a new form of cocaine. In some places, particularly on the West Coast, it is called "rock." Crack, or rock, is smoked, rather than sniffed through the nose or injected, which are the other ways cocaine is taken. Users inhale the vapors that are given off when the crack is heated.

Crack is usually sold in tiny, clear-plastic vials with colorful lids. The vials look like the large capsules vitamins sometimes come in. The crack itself is small white, gray, or beige chunks or crystals that are called "rocks." They look like pieces of soap. In fact, some crack dealers sell soap instead of crack if they think they can get away with it. There are usually three rocks in a vial.

Crack does not burn. To give off its vapors, it must be heated to a high temperature. Some users break the chunks into tiny bits and sprinkle them on marijuana joints or tobacco cigarettes. Then, when they smoke the joint or cigarette, they inhale the crack fumes at the same time.

Most other users smoke the crack in a special water pipe. They place the rocks on a fine steel screen in the pipe and heat the pipe, usually with a small, hand-held gas heater. This melts the crack crystals, releasing the drug vapors.

Whichever way the crack is heated, the user then breathes in, or inhales, the vapors. The drug goes to the lungs. From the lungs, it passes into the bloodstream and reaches the brain within seconds. Immediately, the user gets the special sensations that crack brings.

Crack can be purchased in small amounts. The usual price is about $10 per vial. Some dealers get as little as $5 or as much as $240 for the drug. Each vial

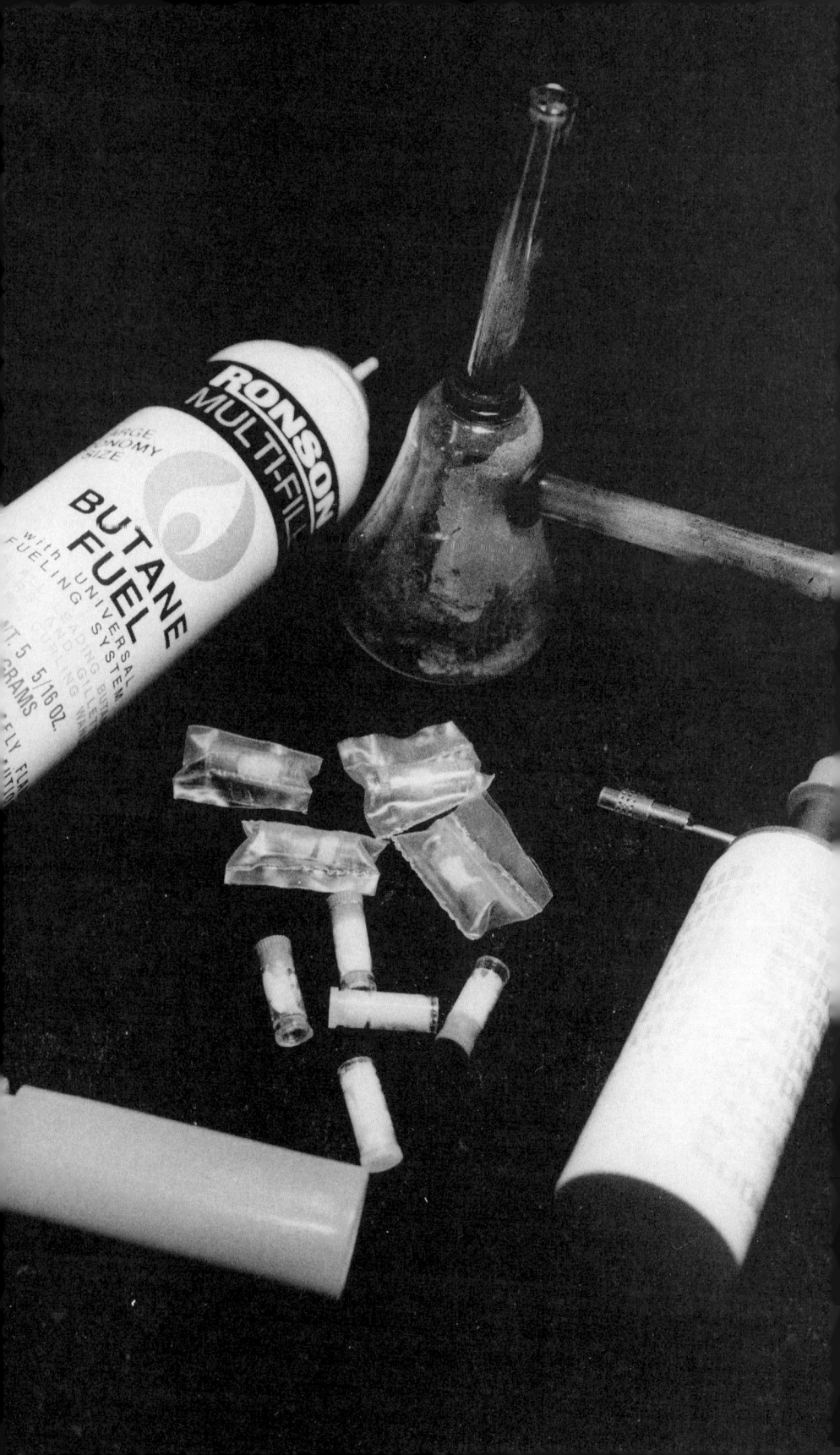

contains about 300 milligrams. Normally that is enough crack for two "hits" or "fixes."

Crack first appeared on the streets of New York City in the summer of 1985. Lieutenant Joe E. Lisi, commanding officer of the Narcotics Division Special Project Unit of the New York City Police Department, reported in February 1986, "Ever since the first vials were discovered last summer, crack is appearing all over the place and in increasing quantities." He estimates that more than half of the cocaine confiscated in New York City is crack. In some neighborhoods, he continued, "90 percent of the cocaine seized is crack." No one knows exactly where crack use began. The most likely place is either New York City or Los Angeles.

Three explanations exist for its name. The most common is that it comes from the crackling noise it makes when it is heated. Some say it is called crack because it resembles cracked bits of plaster that break away from tenement walls. Or perhaps the name refers to the way large chunks of crack are broken into the tiny pieces that fit into a vial.

Crack is the strongest and most powerful type of cocaine now available. As Sterling Johnson, Jr., special New York State drug prosecutor, put it, crack is to cocaine as the atom bomb is to a bomb filled with TNT. Therefore, to understand crack, we must first take a close look at cocaine.

Paraphernalia for smoking crack (capsules in center), including a glass pipe, torch, and lighter

COCAINE: THE "FEEL GOOD" DRUG

Cocaine is found in the leaves of the coca plant (scientific name, *Erythroxylon coca*). The coca bush grows wild in the valleys of the Andes Mountains. It grows as tall as 6 feet (1.8 m) and is covered with shiny, oval-shaped, greenish-brown leaves. According to the National Institute on Drug Abuse (NIDA), the Indians of Peru, Bolivia, and other countries along the Andes Mountains of South America have been chewing the leaves of the coca plant for at least 2,000 years. They use it as a stimulant—to get renewed strength and energy, to ward off the cold of the mountains, to reduce their appotites, and treat a wide variety of diseases.

When the Spanish conquistadores came to South America early in the sixteenth century, they noticed the inhabitants chewing the coca leaves. So they tried doing the same. Although they enjoyed the effect, they were even happier to see the Indians using the cocaine. With it, the Indians worked harder, tired less quickly, and required less food and water. The coca plant thus became very valuable in helping the Spaniards enslave the Indians. Ultimately it led to the Spanish conquest of South America.

Unknown at the time were some healthful effects of the coca plant. As Dr. Ronald K. Siegel of UCLA points out, 100 grams (3.5 oz) of coca leaves contains more than 300 calories and significant amounts of vitamins A and B_2. For people with limited, nutritionally poor diets, this was of benefit.

Other values of cocaine were found after the coca leaf was introduced into Europe early in the nineteenth century. In 1860, the German chemist Albert Niemann succeeded in extracting pure cocaine from the coca leaves. Cocaine, it was discovered, is a powerful pain killer, yet it does not cloud or dull the mind.

When prescribed for patients who were in great pain, it relieved suffering and eased discomfort. Added to cough medicines, nasal sprays, and salves, it treated a host of ailments.

One of the most prominent users of cocaine was Sigmund Freud, the father of psychoanalysis. As well as using it for pleasure, he recommended it to others to relieve depression and fatigue, to control asthma and digestive disorders, and to treat addictions to alcohol or morphine.

In the 1880s, because of its "feel good" qualities, French chemist Angelo Mariani added a bit of cocaine to wine, which he called *Vin Mariani*. Many prominent people, from Pope Leo XIII to Thomas Edison, President McKinley, and actress Sarah Bernhardt, offered testimonials to the qualities of this new drink.

In 1886 a chemist in Georgia, John Styth Pemberton, concocted a drink that he offered as a tonic and general home remedy for headaches and other ailments. Included in the ingredients were both cocaine and caffeine. He called it Coca-Cola. It was not until 1903 that the cocaine was actually removed from this popular soft drink.

While cocaine was being added to drinks to give them an extra kick, doctors continued to find the drug useful in their work. Research studies confirmed that the drug cut down on fatigue and hunger. They also showed that it caused numbness of the nasal passages when sniffed. This suggested that it could be used as a local anesthetic, to kill pain in just one part of the body. Dr. Carl Koller, who was looking for a local anesthetic to use for eye surgery, discovered that it did indeed allow operations on the eye without general anesthesia.

Cocaine was also discovered to be useful in closing up or tightening blood vessels. In medical terms, it is a vasoconstrictor. It proved of great value to surgeons who used it in operations where excessive bleeding was a problem. The cocaine both anesthetized the patient and helped to control the loss of blood.

THE BAD NEWS

As chewed by the Peruvian Indians, the coca leaves presented few problems. The cocaine entered their stomachs. Stomach acids neutralized the full effect of the substance. No one got hooked on the drug; no one died of an overdose.

But when used as a pure drug, the hazards of cocaine soon became obvious. Several states quickly outlawed its use, except for medicinal purposes. In 1908, an amendment to the Pure Food and Drug Act prohibited the interstate shipment of cocaine. The 1914 Harrison Narcotics Act completely banned its use, except under a doctor's supervision. (Cocaine is not a narcotic, but it was included in the act.) And international agreements, signed in 1925 and 1931, made it a crime for any nation to trade in cocaine.

For a while these measures effectively cut the use of cocaine. Peru and Bolivia, the two major growing areas for the coca plant, did not have the laboratories to refine the coca leaves. They found it difficult to ship large, bulky bales of coca leaves, which were easily intercepted. Also, the introduction of other stimulants, such as amphetamines in the 1930s, gave users the same effects as cocaine without the difficulties of transporting the substance.

But the closing of illegal amphetamine laboratories in the late 1960s gave rise to a new demand for cocaine. The cocaine that was bought and sold was very expensive and rather diluted. The drug became popular with many wealthy people and prominent figures in the sports and entertainment fields.

Dr. Robert Byck of the Yale University School of Medicine testified before Congress in 1979 that the high cost and poor quality of cocaine were saving many users from the full consequences of their habit. Street cocaine is almost never pure. Between the original source and the user, the cocaine passes through many hands. And at each step along the way, the purity is "cut," or diluted, by adding other, cheaper substances to the cocaine powder.

For years cocaine largely escaped the bad reputation of other illegal drugs. Although few actually believed that cocaine was harmless, threats from this "champagne of drugs" were far from the concerns of most American families. Cocaine might be a problem for movie stars and rich jet-setters, but not neighborhood kids.

Such ideas began changing with the appearance of crack in its smokable form. Cheap enough to attract even teenagers on an allowance, it is already spreading from the big cities to the suburbs.

3
USERS OF CRACK

Mary was an A student in an inner-city Chicago high school. But she felt "empty inside." Her first experience with drugs came when she was fourteen years old, smoking pot that she bought at a newspaper stand near her school. After a while she began snorting cocaine. From there it was a small step to smoking crack.

About crack, Mary says, "I liked it. It made me feel energetic. But after you got high for a while, you felt depressed. Then you had to get more, and after a while you had to keep on getting more and more."

As Mary's habit grew stronger, she needed $100 or more a day to pay for the drug. To get the money, Mary dropped out of school. She drifted into a life of prostitution. Night after night she came up with different excuses for sleeping away from home. Although her father suspected she was not going to school, he didn't check up.

Mary's life grew increasingly difficult. The dealer who was supplying her with crack began to beat her. She spent more and more of her time "on the pipe." "I got high and then I slept. I ate a Twinkie or two. After a while I didn't even know what day it was."

Crack's extreme addictiveness quickly changes a person's life, often from one of family, friends, and work to one of emotional extremes, crime, and illness that can lead to death.

When Mary realized she was going to have a baby, she called the National Cocaine Hotline, 800-COCAINE. The person who answered the phone gave her a hospital number to call. Even though she got good medical care from then on, her baby was born exposed to drugs. He died soon after birth. Mary is now in treatment and living in a shelter with other girls who are addicted to crack. Every day she struggles to master her strong urge to use crack "just one more time."

In some ways, Mary is a typical user of crack. She's young and bright but risked it all for crack. Teenagers like Mary comprise a large part of the crack population.

800-COCAINE

Much information on users of crack and cocaine has come from the 800-COCAINE hotline. Begun in 1983 by Dr. Mark S. Gold, the hotline gives callers the opportunity to discuss the drug, get questions answered, or ask for help. Dr. Gold had two purposes in mind in setting up the service. One was to offer free help to all those who had cocaine-related problems. The other was to collect information on drug users.

In an article that appeared in the journal *Psychosomatics,* Dr. Gold presented the results of interviews with several hundred randomly selected callers to the number.

According to the study, about 85 percent of cocaine users were white and around thirty years old. Although most callers ranged in age from twenty-five to forty, the youngest was eighteen and the oldest seventy-eight.

Most callers said expense was the only limitation on their use of cocaine. Fewer than 10 percent said that illness, either physical or mental, had ever led them to stop the drug use.

Dr. Mark S. Gold, who set up the 800-COCAINE hotline

Although men were thought to be the main abusers of cocaine, Dr. Gold and his co-workers were surprised to find that about one-third of the callers were women. In general, the abusers had at least a few years of college and many were professionals—doctors, lawyers, engineers, teachers, airline pilots, and business people. An average income of $25,000 placed them at a rather high economic level. Their cocaine habit had begun a little less than five years before they called the hotline. A full 90 percent first got involved by snorting cocaine.

Overall, Dr. Gold's findings show that occasional users quickly increased the frequency and quantity of cocaine that they took until they became dependent on the drug. Men and women who had been honest, law-abiding citizens before getting hooked on cocaine robbed and stole to pay for the drug. And many who had once enjoyed good health were now suffering a variety of physical and mental ailments springing from their cocaine use.

The leading physical problems that were reported to Dr. Gold were, in order: insomnia, fatigue, severe headaches, damage to the nasal passages for snorters, poor sexual performance, seizures or loss of consciousness, and nausea and vomiting.

Over 80 percent of the users described three main psychological problems—depression, anxiety, and irritability. Among the other symptoms that came up frequently were paranoia (delusions of being persecuted), loss of interest in nondrug activities, inability to concentrate, and estrangement from friends and family. Thirty-eight percent thought of committing suicide, and 9 percent actually tried!

A full 73 percent of the callers said that they could not control their desire for cocaine nor limit its use. Just over 60 percent considered themselves addicts. As a measure of their craving for cocaine, 72 percent considered the drug more important than their families, 71 percent preferred cocaine to food, 69 percent put cocaine ahead of friends, and 50 percent thought cocaine more vital than sex.

The cocaine habit also caused difficulties beyond the physical and psychological. Twelve percent had been arrested either for dealing or possession of the drug. About half admitted stealing money, and about the same number had used up most of their savings and were in debt. Nearly 40 percent had career difficulties; 17 percent had been fired from their jobs. More than half were either divorced or threatened with divorce as a result of drug use.

When asked why they took cocaine, 82 percent said they did it for the euphoria, or high, that it provided. Fifty-seven percent said that it relieved the boredom of their daily lives. And 48 percent said that the drug gave them more energy and self-confidence.

Dr. Gold now finds that 40 percent of the users who call the hotline are smoking crack. His figures show that the average age of crack users is about seventeen. Nearly half are under twenty-five.

Each year a government agency, the National Institute on Drug Abuse, conducts a National Household Survey on Drug Abuse. In 1991 the study found that most current users of crack were between the ages of eighteen and thirty-four and almost 50 percent were white, 36 percent were black, and 14 percent were Hispanic. The vast majority of current crack users are male—82 percent.

WHY CRACK?

Younger persons are being turned on to this deadly drug for several reasons. One is that crack is relatively cheap. A $10 vial is enough for two hits. Some teenagers begin to support their habit with money from their allowance and a part-time job.

Despite the low initial cost, however, crack can

become very expensive. The high is very short-lived and "sets up the craving again and again," says Dan Langdon, former director of public information for Phoenix House, a drug treatment center in New York City. In comparison with snorting a line of cocaine powder, a crack user "hits the pipe four to six times in the same amount of time." A habitual user is soon spending hundreds of dollars a day.

Crack is also easy to use. As Mark Raskin, a former TV producer who suffered from a crack addiction, once explained, "It's like instant coffee. Prefabricated."

People with limited drug experience seem to be less afraid of taking a few puffs on a pipe or cigarette than of popping pills or injecting themselves. Many are especially frightened of contracting AIDS, a devastating disease that can be passed from person to person by using the same unsterilized hypodermic needle.

Users know that crack is much purer than street cocaine powder. This offers some protection against getting sick from what is called a "bad cut," meaning impure or disease-causing adulterants in the drug.

Finally, the word on the street is that crack gives a stronger, better high and is sexually stimulating. Ironically, its effects often prove to be exactly the opposite. The end result is often frigidity or impotence.

Dr. Gold estimates that about a million Americans have smoked crack at least once. Forty-five percent of males arrested in Los Angeles tested positive for crack and cocaine. Crack-cocaine was involved in 32 percent of New York City homicides, and 60 percent of all drug-related homicides in the city. From January through April 1986, while police seizures of marijuana and heroin fell off by around 90 percent, crack and cocaine seizures rose 41 percent.

The rapid spread of crack leads some experts to

fear a new wave of cocaine addiction in the United States. The 1991 National Household Survey on Drug Abuse, a government study of 75 million U.S. residents, found that 3.9 million had used crack at least once, and half a million had used crack within the past month. A third of the adult population knows someone who uses crack or cocaine.

GETTING HOOKED

Encounters with cocaine or crack usually occur first in social situations. Classmates get their school friends started with some free "hits." At parties and in clubs and bars, nonusers may be put under pressure to "go along with the crowd." And in offices, stores, and factories, workers offer the drug to fellow workers to help them through particularly difficult days.

"What's the big deal?" asked one young crack user. "Everyone tries it at least once. A single snort or smoke can't hurt."

Three possible courses follow that first exposure. Some may lay off the drug and never try it again. "It doesn't do anything for me. Who needs all the expense? Who wants to risk getting busted? Forget it!"

Some others may enjoy the feelings they got from the drug and try to use it occasionally. Although a few succeed in using cocaine this way, most crack users learn that crack is not a recreational drug. It is extremely rare to find someone who uses it only now and then.

The majority of people who try crack for the first time become dependent on the substance within days or weeks. They crave crack all the time. With increasing frequency and growing amounts they try to maintain the euphoria that the substance gives them.

The risks of getting hooked on crack are far greater than with other forms of cocaine. Users who

Many crack addicts suffer from drinking problems too.

once snorted cocaine occasionally say that after switching to crack they increased their use to three or four times a week. Experts have found that while many cocaine addicts manage to maintain their jobs, it is almost impossible for crack addicts to keep up their normal lives. They undergo personality changes, especially paranoia, and their relationships often fall apart. They get into trouble at work.

Many crack addicts may suffer from drinking problems, too, a difficulty that is not widely known. "Almost all cocaine patients are in trouble with drinking," says one social worker who counsels crack addicts. "They use alcohol to bring themselves down off the cocaine high." She explains that addicts use alcohol to ease the often devastating crash that follows a cocaine high.

Even when people on cocaine or crack realize they have a problem, or become frightened by the highly publicized deaths of people like Len Bias or Don Rogers, it's not always easy for them to seek treatment. They know the drug is bad for them, but they lust after the powerful euphoria produced by crack. Users often say crack makes them feel "on top of the world."

Some social scientists believe that American society may promote abuse of drugs. The message that it gives out is that "taking something" to make you feel better is perfectly acceptable. What is not acceptable is to endure any sort of pain or discomfort. Almost every home has an array of remedies to be taken at the first signs of distress. Tense? Take a pill. Unhappy? Have a drink. Want to relax? Light a cigarette.

It is a small jump from this way of thinking to cocaine and crack abuse. Personal problems are forgotten when under the influence of the drug. Unfortunately, crack is so addictive, so toxic, and so physically harmful that it soon consumes most users' lives.

4
DANGERS OF CRACK

People who knew David before he started smoking crack do not recognize him. Once handsome, he is now thin and gaunt. Most of the time he finds it hard to sit still, talks nonstop, and has his hands and legs in constant motion.

When he is not abnormally active, David becomes sullen and withdrawn. He often feels his heart pounding in his chest. A few times he has suffered seizures and fallen to the floor unconscious. He finds it difficult to sleep at night. When he closes his eyes, he feels creatures crawling on his skin and fears imaginary beasts that seem about to attack him.

David speaks of his addiction to crack. "I really liked it," he recalls, "even though the peak high lasted just a few minutes and cost me up to $200 a night."

Although David could see what was happening to him, he felt that "none of it mattered." His craving for the drug led him to smoke pipe after pipe until he passed out.

David doubts that he will ever be able to put back together the pieces of his life as a successful bank manager. When asked what advice he would give those considering crack for the first time, he said, "Don't even start. It makes life too damn difficult."

Doctors who practice medicine in New York City's Bellevue Hospital substance abuse program see firsthand how all of the ill effects associated with cocaine—seizures, paranoia, high blood pressure, heart disorders, and weight loss—are significantly more intense with crack.

As was said earlier, when crack is smoked, the vapors go into the lungs, where they are immediately absorbed by the bloodstream. A large, concentrated dose of the drug reaches the brain within seconds. Doctors agree that this is perhaps the most efficient way to take a drug. It produces a quick and intense reaction.

Cocaine is a stimulant. It is different from heroin, for example, which is a depressant. Crack addicts are likely to be highly active and anxious, therefore, as compared to heroin addicts, who are generally lethargic and quiet.

The stimulating effects of crack begin within ten seconds, which is as long as it takes to reach the brain. Crack is so concentrated in its action that when it reaches the brain users often describe the sensation as "an explosion."

With the very first puffs of crack, the user begins to feel very good, even euphoric. Users call this sensation a "flash" or a "rush." The feeling is accompanied by a sense of strength and power, exhilaration, and the ability to succeed at any task. Fatigue and hunger disappear.

The impact of crack on the central nervous system also tends to make users very talkative; often they will chatter away whether or not they have something to say. The drug also tightens the body's blood vessels, raising blood pressure up as high as 10 to 20 percent above normal. This increases the danger of a brain hemorrhage, a burst blood vessel in the brain. A higher body temperature also results.

The pupils of the eyes dilate, or open larger. This sometimes makes objects appear fuzzy, with a halo around them. So common is this reaction that users have given the halo a name; they call it a "snowlight." Users also report an excessive sensitivity to light and spots before the eyes.

The heartbeat picks up a lot of speed. Doctors report increases in the range of 30 to 50 percent. The danger of heart attack is greater with this abnormally fast heartbeat. A December 1992 report from the Bureau of Justice Statistics indicated that a single dose of cocaine can cause convulsion or death due to heart failure. Large quantities of cocaine can interrupt the user's normal heart rhythm, cause a heart attack, and result in death. In 1990, cocaine was involved in more drug-related deaths than any other single illegal drug—43 percent.

Crack makes the heart muscles more sensitive to the natural stimulant adrenaline, which the body produces. Adrenaline normally makes the heart beat faster. With crack in the system, the heart muscles begin to twitch and are unable to pump blood. Frequently the result is death.

Something similar happens when the crack reaches the brain cells. The user may begin to shake and tremble with convulsions. Sometimes there is a loss of control over arms and legs; limbs jerk and move about despite all attempts to keep them still. In many cases the result is seizures, a condition in which the person becomes stiff and unmoving and loses consciousness.

Regular users often neglect eating, either because of being on a high or having spent all their money on the drug. Malnutrition usually follows a rapid and considerable weight loss. Dr. Mark Gold has conducted research that seems to show deficiencies of vitamins B_6 and C among habitual users of crack.

The effects of crack last only a short time, no more than fifteen minutes. (By contrast, the high from snorting powder cocaine may last up to an hour.) As the effects begin to wear off, the user goes into a depression that is more intense than the euphoria of the flash. They call this "crashing." The user feels very tired, irritable, and depressed. Sometimes there are even some temporary symptoms of mental disorder. This is followed by an overwhelming craving for more cocaine. As one user says when he's crashing, "I'd kill for it!"

The user can relieve the effects of the crash by taking another dose of cocaine. Because the high from smokable cocaine is so short compared to the high from powder cocaine, users repeat the experience with greater frequency. This leads to faster abuse and addiction. And it more often results in hours of continuous use, called "binges," followed by complete physical collapse.

PSYCHOLOGICAL EFFECTS

Hallucinations are normal for crack users. Crack smokers hear sounds and see things that do not exist. They hear laughter coming from empty rooms; they see heavy pieces of furniture moving and swaying. Among the most frequent hallucinations is the sensation that little insects are crawling around on or under the skin. This feeling is so common that users have given it a name, "cocaine bugs."

Paranoia is another psychological consequence. Crack users suffer from the delusion that they are surrounded by enemies and people out to hurt or kill them. A noise at night may make users think that FBI agents have come to arrest them or a drug dealer is at the door to collect an unpaid debt. The fear that telephones are bugged or spies are lurking about is not uncommon. One habitual user, convinced that someone out to kill him was in the trunk of his car, fired several shots into the rear of the auto while speeding along a highway!

There are also other signs of emotional distress. A loss of interest in family and friends leads to feelings of loneliness and isolation. Sex often loses its appeal, as does the drive to succeed. All too often, users drop their sense of what is moral and ethical. A longtime crack abuser, Linda, changed from being an honest, churchgoing wife and mother to hustling crack on the streets of Los Angeles.

Even though cocaine is a stimulant and energizes the body, chronic use of the drug has the very opposite effect. Instead of euphoria and a feeling of well-being, the user experiences dysphoria, that is, low energy, depression, sluggishness of movement, and a noticeable lack of emotion.

Some experts believe that the drug interferes with a certain chemical messenger in the brain known as dopamine. Dopamine is thought to be associated with pleasurable feelings, alertness, and control of body movements. It carries messages by moving from one brain cell to another.

After the dopamine has gone to the second cell, some of it is broken down into other chemicals. Some, though, heads back to the first cell. The cocaine, however, blocks the return. Because it can't get back, the effect of the dopamine is multiplied. The cocaine user's high, then, is caused by the buildup of dopamine between the brain cells.

In time, though, the dopamine without a home is also broken down by the body. The good feelings disappear, to be replaced by depression, anxiety, and a powerful hunger for more cocaine. This is the crash that follows the original euphoria.

Cocaine also interferes with the brain's production

of another chemical, serotonin. Serotonin is responsible for sleep. Just in order to be able to fall asleep, habitual users of cocaine will turn to other drugs, such as alcohol, marijuana, sedatives, and heroin, or will increase their use of cocaine.

CRACK ADDICTION

Dr. Mark Gold defines addiction as "an irresistible compulsion to use the drug at increasing doses and frequency even in the face of serious physical and psychological side effects and the extreme disruption of the user's personal relationships and system of values." Speaking specifically about crack, Dr. Gold has said, "The use of cocaine in this form appears to cause a more rapid addiction and severe changes in the brain chemistry. It is the fast and more potent action that makes crack more physically harmful."

For a long time people had the false belief that cocaine was not addictive. It was said that users could enjoy its phenomenal high without consequences. But experience and research show something else. They make it clear that many people do, in fact, become addicted to cocaine.

OVERDOSE

The tolerance for a drug is the amount that can be taken without suffering the ill effects of an overdose. The tolerance for cocaine and crack, like that for alcohol, varies widely from person to person. It has generally been accepted that the smallest dose of cocaine that can kill a person is 1.2 grams taken within twenty-four hours. Yet some doctors have reported treating patients who have taken over 10 grams—and survived. And there are accounts of some people who have taken amounts measuring a few thousandths of a gram—and died.

But cocaine has a very narrow margin of safety. If someone takes just a tiny bit more than his or her limit, the person suffers the effects of an overdose. The symptoms start as soon as the use level goes above a certain point. Irritability, anxiety, lack of good judgment, and some mental confusion follow a mild overdose. The addicts may find themselves picking at imaginary bugs and snakes on their skin, grinding their teeth, or losing their motor coordination.

Chronic users sometimes experience something that they call "kindling." This occurs when they take just a small amount of cocaine, yet have a very strong, completely unexpected reaction. The most frequent results of kindling are convulsions, seizures, or some form of psychotic behavior. Researchers think that kindling may be caused by changes in the brain cells due to longtime cocaine use.

A report in the journal *Psychopharmacologia* described an experiment in which scientists allowed laboratory monkeys to have as many injections of cocaine as they wanted by simply working a lever. Some monkeys took the drug almost without stop, ignoring food and water. Within five days they were all dead.

Few humans use cocaine in this way. But craving for the drug can be an extremely serious problem for those who do get started.

PRENATAL EXPOSURE

Guillermo is a newborn baby, just one week old, at Broward General Medical Center in Fort Lauderdale, Florida. His mother is an abuser of crack, and the doctors say that Guillermo was actually born exposed to crack. (NOTE: Experts say babies are only born addicted to heroin.)

Small and underweight, Guillermo cries most of the time he is awake. He is tense and jittery. When someone touches him, no matter how gently, his tiny body trembles. His eyes don't focus. And he doesn't even have the natural instinct to suck that is common to all healthy babies.

A fetus that is exposed to cocaine often will not grow according to schedule. It may have strokes and seizures, and can be born with malformed kidneys, genitals, intestines, and spinal cord. Children who have been exposed to cocaine in the womb frequently exhibit a variety of neurological and behavioral problems when they reach school age. These children cannot focus their attention on their teachers or their studies for any extended period of time, have trouble learning new skills, and find it difficult to follow instructions. They also tend to misbehave, and often pick fights with other students.

Because of the epidemic of crack that is currently sweeping the country, the number of infants born to cocaine addicts has been skyrocketing. A 1988 study of U.S. hospitals found that at least 11 percent of the pregnant women surveyed had exposed their unborn fetuses to illegal drugs, with cocaine being the most common drug. The President's National Drug Control Strategy Report, published in 1992, estimated that 100,000 crack-exposed infants are born every year. The March of Dimes has predicted that as many as 4 million drug-exposed children will be attending school by the year 2000. The problem in the inner cities is expected to be even worse, with up to 60 percent of all inner-city children suffering the effects of prenatal exposure to drugs.

A number of crack babies are not able to survive the first few months of life. At best, they require intensive care in the neonatal nursery. The cost of caring for a prenatally cocaine-exposed infant far exceeds the average cost of treating a newborn. One study conducted at an inner-city hospital in New York City found that the cost of newborn care jumped from $2,757 to $7,957 when the baby had been exposed to cocaine before birth, and the newborn's stay in the hospital increased from 5.1 days to 11.5 days.

In New York City's Harlem, Mother Clara Hale founded Hale House in 1969 to care for the babies of drug addicts. Until 1985, not one infant died while in her care. In 1985, though, three crack babies died. As Mother Hale once said, "These crack babies are so young and so small. They're just dying on me."

There is however, reason for hope. Studies have shown that many of the behavioral and learning problems that affect large numbers of children exposed to crack-cocaine before birth can be overcome when the children are helped by trained professionals. Under the care of trained teachers, these children have learned how to control their aggressive behavior toward other children and develop age-appropriate reading, writing, and speaking skills. Unfortunately, according to a 1992 article published by the National Institute on Drug Abuse, the problems of so-called "crack kids" are complicated by poor nutrition, abusive family relationships, and prenatal exposure to smoke and alcohol.

WITHDRAWAL

Withdrawal is the process of stopping drug use and the unpleasant reactions it causes. With many addictive drugs, withdrawal leads to a set of rather severe physical and psychological symptoms that most former users experience. Withdrawal from habitual, heavy crack use produces reactions that are different from those suffered by people addicted to other drugs.

At first the person attempting to withdraw from

Clara Hale of Hale House, a group foster home in Harlem, New York City, for infants of drug addicts

crack experiences an intense craving for the drug. Every waking moment is filled with thoughts about the drug—how good it felt, how much it is missed, and how great it would be to get just one more crack fix. Along with the powerful, all-consuming desire for more crack come irritability, depression, apathy, fuzzy thinking, and varied sleep disorders. These strong and powerful symptoms last from a few days to two weeks.

At this point, the reactions fade away. They are replaced by a phase often called the "honeymoon." Instead of the distress of the early days, there are now strong feelings of relief and self-satisfaction. "I've broken the habit. I'm in control of my life. I've fought and won the most difficult battle of my life!"

But the honeymoon does not last very long. Soon the person again becomes aware of the pleasure that he or she is missing. There may also be some continuing difficulty in thinking clearly, along with general feelings of tension and anxiety. These confused and conflicting sensations may go on for a very long time. Some say that the desire for the drug never disappears completely.

EFFECTS ON SOCIETY

In some ways it is easier to measure the effects of crack on the user than to assess the damage to the family. The huge amounts of money needed to support a crack habit can lead to financial ruin. And the behavior patterns of the user—both because of the drug's mood-altering qualities and the desperate search for a hit when crashing—can tear people, marriages, families, and friendships apart.

With crack sweeping the nation, society at large is suffering as much as the addicts and their families. The drain on our nation's wealth and the loss of our economic edge to the Japanese has been blamed, in part, on substance abuse. In 1991 the Federal government devoted more than $10.8 billion of its budget to controlling illegal drugs. Between 1981 and 1991 the Federal drug control budget increased almost sevenfold. Crime is a major problem in almost every city, and in suburban and rural areas as well. Police statistics show that drugs are implicated in more than half of these crimes. Nearly half of the record 1,867 murders committed in New York City in 1988 were related to the use of crack. Robberies, burglaries, and muggings are often committed by addicts seeking the money to support their drug habit. Even more dismaying, the illegal drug trade has created an immense underworld of drug traffickers and dealers to whom crime is a daily way of life.

Children who were exposed to crack in the womb are also racking up huge bills for medical treatment. Large sums of money have to be pumped into the public school system as these children, who pose special educational and disciplinary challenges, reach school age. Since cocaine-exposed children can lead reasonably normal lives if there is early intervention by specially trained professionals, the money society must devote to rehabilitation and treatment is well-spent.

Users are unabl 'o their jobs, so there is a breakdown in produ nd services. A 1990 government study found ... workers who had used cocaine had twice the absentee rate of employees who did not use cocaine.

Increased medical treatment costs result in rising taxes and higher health insurance premiums for all. Crack-cocaine use has been associated with the same high-risk behaviors that can lead to sexually transmitted diseases, including syphilis and acquired immunodeficiency syndrome (AIDS). A 1990 survey of black teenage crack users in California found that they had significantly increased rates of high-risk behavior, such as having many different sexual partners and inadequate use of condoms, compared with the general population. Other studies conducted by the Centers for Disease Control and Prevention (CDC) found a connection between the rise in crack addiction and the increased number of syphilis cases. In one area of Georgia, the incidence of syphilis rose 800 percent between 1985 and 1989. We are also more liable to be hurt or killed in auto accidents because drugs and driving are a deadly combination. Our police departments, courts, and jails are being stretched to the breaking point as they try to cope with the crack epidemic.

We are living through a real national crisis—a waste of life and money, an erosion of law and peace. It is a little like being at war. Crack can destroy our society just as surely as an enemy attacking our nation!

5
MANUFACTURE AND SALE OF CRACK

His name was José Santa Cruz Londono. On the street he was known as Santa Cruz. The U.S. Attorney's Office in Brooklyn, New York, considered him one of the largest suppliers of cocaine and crack in New York. Born in 1944, Santa Cruz was slightly over 6 feet (1.8 m) tall and weighed about 210 pounds (95 kg). A dropout from high school, Santa Cruz commanded an organization that extended from his native Colombia to the street corners of New York.

The Santa Cruz group owned several factories in Colombia that prepared cocaine powder. It owned four or five airplanes and employed as many as ten pilots to transport the cocaine. Cruz's distribution network also included ten lieutenants in New York, Miami, Los Angeles, and other American cities.

Scattered around New York and the other cities in which Santa Cruz operated were dozens of apartments and houses with underground storage vaults. Here he kept the supplies of cocaine, as well as caches of pistols, automatic weapons, and quantities of ammunition. Several corporations served as fronts to the whole operation. The profits were deposited into a bank in Panama that Santa Cruz controlled.

Authorities said that Santa Cruz distributors sold about a ton of cocaine for $51 million in a three-year period. Once it reached the street level, the cocaine was worth several hundred million dollars.

FROM COCA TO COCAINE

The leaves of the coca plant contain fourteen alkaloids. Alkaloids are chemicals known as bases; they contain nitrogen, carbon, oxygen, and hydrogen. One of these bases is cocaine. Its full, jaw-breaking name is 2-beta-carbomethoxy-3-beta-benzoxytropane. The cocaine makes up only about 1 percent by weight of all the chemicals in the coca leaf.

The basic preparation of the cocaine for street use is almost always handled in the countries where the coca is grown. First the coca leaves are dried in the sun. Then they are placed either in a press or in a steel drum. Sulfuric acid and kerosene are added, and the leaves are crushed or mashed. The result is called coca paste, which contains cocaine sulfate.

The coca paste is then usually shipped to Colombia and sold to one of the drug lords there, who operate many small cocaine manufacturing laboratories. In these labs ether, alcohol, and hydrochloric acid are

Coca farmers in Colombia picking the coca leaves off the trees. The trees grow to 7 feet (2.1 m) high and can be picked every three months. Coca farming is a very profitable business in parts of South America.

Above: *in this open-air laboratory in Colombia, a farmer spreads the harvested coca leaves on a plastic sheet, to let the leaves dry in the sun.* Right: *one of the lab workers empties the tobacco from a cigarette wrapper. He will use the wrapper to roll up the coca "paste," which is sitting to his left and which he has previously prepared and taste-tested.*

added to the paste. Known as solvents, these chemicals dissolve and remove impurities in the paste. The result is crystals of cocaine hydrochloride.

In the last step of processing, the crystals are ground into a white, odorless powder that is ready to be sold to the big, international drug distributors. It takes about 2.5 pounds (1.1 kg) of coca paste to make 1 pound (0.45 kg) of cocaine hydrochloride.

Most of the street cocaine prepared in Colombian laboratories is sold in the United States. An army of "runners" has the job of smuggling the drug here. These runners all work for the big drug lords. Small boats and planes are pressed into service to transport the stuff. Some of it is hidden aboard big passenger ships, freighters, or airliners. The rest may be slipped inside hollowed-out logs, bales of fabrics, tin cans, or anything else that can possibly hold the cocaine—including the suitcases of unsuspecting American tourists who are asked to deliver the package to someone's "sister" in Miami.

No matter how they do it, the runners get the cocaine into the United States. Once inside the borders, it is delivered to the distributors, who get the cocaine to the local dealers. And it is from here that the cocaine gets passed on to the street dealers. These dealers are often users who depend on the money they earn selling to support their very expensive habit.

In their greed for greater profits, the cocaine dealers seldom sell the pure cocaine. Instead, they "cut" the cocaine. This means that they add other substances, called adulterants, to the cocaine. Common adulterants are flour, baking soda, or talcum powder; sugars, such as lactose (milk sugar), or mannitol (a laxative); local anesthetics, such as procaine (Novocaine), lidocaine (Xylocaine), or benzocaine; and chemicals, such as caffeine or amphetamines.

The adulterants do more than add weight to the

cocaine. They also increase the danger to the drug user. Foreign chemical substances in the cocaine increase the user's chances of suffering a bad reaction. Also, users who become accustomed to adulterated cocaine can become very sick or even die if given pure cocaine. Experts estimate that street cocaine is only between 20 to 60 percent pure.

The cocaine powder sold on the street, known as "coke" or "snow," is usually sniffed or snorted up through the nose. Users place a small quantity, perhaps 25 to 30 milligrams, on a flat, clean, dry, shiny surface such as a small mirror. With a sharp razor blade or knife, they chop the cocaine into an even finer powder. They then arrange it in what is called a "line." A line is about an inch (2.5 cm) long and one-eighth of an inch (0.3 cm) wide. Users snort the line through a drinking straw or a rolled-up dollar bill. They hold one end of the tube in the nose and slowly move the other end over the line, breathing in all the while.

For the coke abuser this method has its drawbacks. It takes several minutes to work, its impact is not as strong as it might be, and in time it destroys the lining of the nose.

Another, less popular way of taking cocaine is by injection. This is said to work faster and bring about a stronger reaction. To inject the cocaine, users dissolve the cocaine powder in water. They then draw the liquid up in a hypodermic needle and inject it, usually into a vein in the arm.

Still another form of cocaine has appeared, called "freebase." The name comes from the fact that the cocaine base is separated, or freed, from the other chemicals in the cocaine powder.

Freebase is prepared by the users, not the dealers. To the powder form of street cocaine, they add water and ammonium hydroxide. This separates the cocaine from the other ingredients. To extract the

Users of cocaine often inhale "lines" of the white powder.

pure cocaine base from the water, they mix in a fast-drying solvent, such as ether. After the ether evaporates, the substance that is left is pure freebase.

Users often try to speed up the evaporation process by heating the mixture. Because ether is highly flammable, this is an extremely dangerous thing to do. It has caused many accidents, such as the explosion that badly injured comedian Richard Pryor in 1980. Pryor was heating the ether when it burst into flames, burning him badly.

Making freebase removes the adulterants and nonactive parts of the cocaine powder. What it leaves is a pure, powerful cocaine base. Freebase is not water soluble; therefore it can't be sniffed or injected. The only way it can be taken is by smoking.

Users smoke freebase in a special water pipe. The bowl has several layers of stainless steel screens. The freebase is placed on the top screen. As the pipe is heated, the substance melts and becomes an oil that gives off vapors. Inhaling the air over the freebase brings the vapors into the smoker's mouth and lungs.

Smoking cocaine freebase is much more dangerous than snorting cocaine powder. The freebase is rapidly absorbed in the lungs and carried to the brain in a few seconds. The result is a sudden and intense high. But just as quickly the user crashes and the good feelings disappear. The user is left with an enormous craving to freebase again and again.

FROM COCAINE TO CRACK

Unlike freebase, crack is prepared by the dealers, not the users, from powder cocaine. The process is very simple. The dealers mix regular street cocaine powder with water and baking soda to make a thick paste.

In Florida, in front of spectators, drug enforcement agents explode a large drum of ether found in a cocaine lab. Ether is a highly flammable substance.

They then heat the paste in a pot on a stove. When it has dried, the material looks like a hunk of soap or a bowl of slightly dirty sugar that has been formed into one solid lump by moisture in the air. Now the dealers break the crack into small chunks, called rocks, and place them in tiny, clear-plastic vials. Each vial usually contains enough crack for two hits.

The dealers making the crack don't need a factory or a laboratory. All they require is a kitchen with a stove. That is why most crack is produced in small apartments rented by the dealers.

Since each dealer makes the crack in a slightly different way, some crack is sold with brand names. This is to help the users identify the crack they are buying. Some brands reported for sale in New York are Fantasy, Imperial, Lucky 7, Snurf, and Mister T.

The New York City police estimate that 60 percent of the cocaine on the streets is in the form of crack. Crack is almost 100 percent pure—far purer than street cocaine. This makes the crack more potent. The crack is also faster-acting. Smoking crack gets the cocaine to the brain within seconds. Snorted cocaine takes three to four minutes to start working.

Crack is far cheaper than other forms of cocaine. A gram of cocaine powder costs around $100. A vial of crack can be bought on the street for $10. This

Comedian Richard Pryor's well-publicized brush with death was, he later admitted, due to cocaine abuse. Pryor burned himself very badly in an accident he suffered while smoking cocaine.

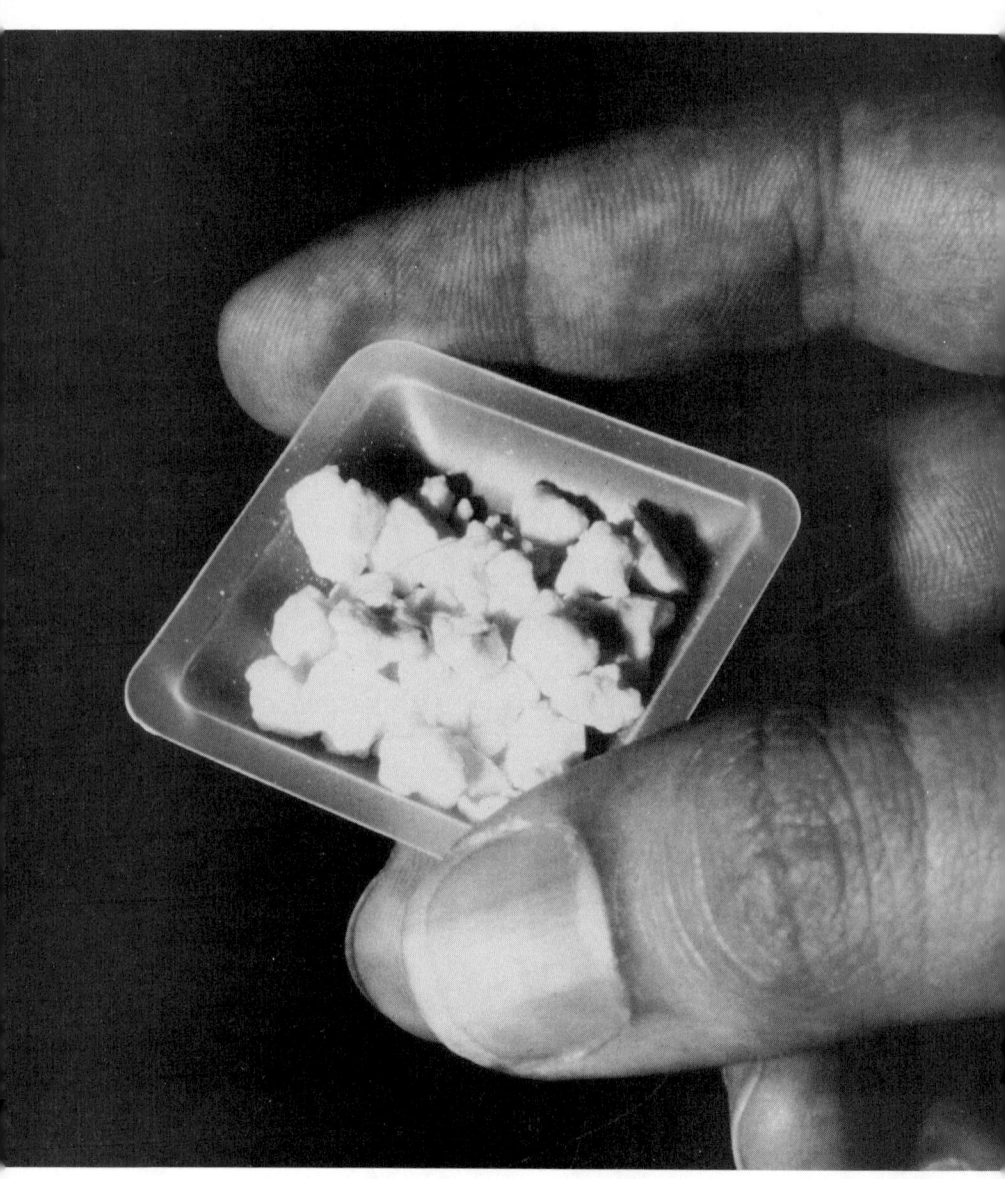
Chunks of crack, often called "rocks"

combination of increased power, a quicker and more intense high, and lower cost has led experts to call crack the "state-of-the-art" drug. It has made crack use explode across the country.

SPACE BASE

Some call it "space base." Others call it "star speed." No matter what the street name, dealers in Los Angeles, New York City, and Baltimore have been peddling this new—and even more dangerous—form of crack.

This high-tech-named drug is a mixture of crack and PCP. PCP is short for phencyclidine. Also called "angel dust," PCP is one of the most powerful of all mind-altering drugs. Users often act bizarrely and become violent, as though suffering from serious mental illness.

The manufacturers of space base either soak rocks of crack in liquid PCP or sprinkle them with PCP powder. This lethal mixture is then sold to users who smoke it like crack, on a joint or cigarette, or in a water pipe. Although only a few cases of people taking space base have been reported, doctors say the hybrid drug can produce severe paranoia, seizures, dizziness, hallucinations, and violent, delusional behavior.

Space base is so powerful a drug that one undercover officer, when he bought some in New York City, was told by the dealer, "Be careful with it, because it beams you up too fast." A counsellor at Odyssey House, a New York City drug treatment center, once reported, "We've gotten about three or four kids who say that's what they've taken. But I don't think it will ever be too popular. It's just too dangerous."

CRACK ON THE STREET

Habitual users buy their crack from street dealers or in special places called crack houses (called rock houses on the West Coast). Often located in dirty and rundown parts of town, they may be set in abandoned buildings or stores. At times they are located in busy neighborhood apartments or storefronts where heavy day and night traffic will pass unnoticed by residents or the police. The houses are open to anyone who looks like he or she wants a fix and is not suspected to be an undercover narcotics agent.

Studies of drug use in the inner city of Detroit, Michigan, noted that there are actually two types of crack houses. One is classified as the "buy, get high, and party" type of crack house, where users consume crack and engage in other social activities, often sexual, at the same location. The other class of crack house is commonly called the "hole-in-the-wall." Here the crack buyer places money through a small opening, receives the drug, and then goes to another location to use the drug.

Barricades or other barriers may block off the buildings housing the crack houses, and serve as a first line of protection in case of a police raid. Strong security systems in the crack houses sometimes include metal bars over the windows, reinforced doors and locks, and armed guards. The safety measures are as much to guard against attacks from within the crack community as to fend off police raids. Since a crack house can make profits of over $20,000 a month, competitors are often at odds out of fear of takeovers by rival operators. Threats and outbreaks of violence are commonplace, sometimes catching innocent victims in the crossfire.

Base houses are places where crack is sold *and*

Police raid a "crack house," battering down the door in search for drugs.

smoked. They are similar to the opium dens of years ago. Only customers who are known to the operators are allowed to enter the base house. The atmosphere inside is quiet and relaxed. Everyone is smoking, or "on the pipe," as they say. Usually the price of the crack is higher where it is smoked on the premises. Sometimes the houses even provide the glass pipes for their customers to use.

Children, unfortunately, play an important role in inner-city drug trade. In North Philadelphia, for example, where crack use is rampant, children as young as eight years old are employed in the drug business. They deliver crack, guard crack houses, shuttle large quantities of money between dealers and suppliers, and perform a variety of other drug-related jobs. Between 1985 and 1987 a street-level drug dealer in Washington, D.C., had a one in seventy chance of getting killed, according to a Rand Corporation study. This risk of getting killed is twenty times higher than the risk faced by a police officer, and a hundred times higher than that faced by someone in the general work force.

Few users stop to think that they are at the end of a long chain of events that starts in the highlands of South America, where the coca plant is grown. The road from there to the streets of our cities is paved with corruption, violence, and organized crime. Not only do users pay the price with *their* lives, they also threaten the welfare and well-being of the rest of society.

CUTTING SUPPLY

It started with a rumor. Someone told someone who told the authorities that Air America, a small airplane charter service in Scranton, Pennsylvania, was involved in drug smuggling. The Drug Enforcement Administration (DEA) decided to check out the report.

"We looked and determined that the company wasn't doing enough business to justify its outlays," said DEA special agent Dennis Molloy. The DEA launched a full-scale investigation.

For five years, they followed the pilots and workers at Air America. They traced flight after flight down to Colombia and back up to tiny landing strips in Pennsylvania, New York, and Florida. The planes were seen taking off with "at least twenty-five duffle bags, each one stuffed with about $1 million." And the same aircraft were observed returning, loaded down with over 1,000 pounds (450 kg) of cocaine from Colombia. It was learned that the pilots were paid as much as $1.5 million for each trip.

When the agents had collected enough evidence to build a case they picked up and arrested five ring members. Warrants were issued for seven more. And the DEA dug up over $4 million in $20 bills buried on the property of the Air America owner.

The federal indictment accused the men of smuggling in 7.5 *tons* of cocaine from Colombia and of laundering $25 million in profits. This drug bust was but one of many. But, as the biggest in the history of drug enforcement, it represents our country's best effort to cut the cocaine supply coming into this country.

CRACKING DOWN

The American public is against drugs. People everywhere seek an end to the crime, violence, and corruption that spring from the black market in powder cocaine and crack. They want to be able to walk the streets without fear of robbery by addicts who need money for their next fix. And they want to see dealers who prey on the young put out of business. Most people think stopping the supply of drugs is the best way to reduce crime, according to the results of a recent Gallup poll. Interestingly, in a Gallup poll taken about ten years ago most people believed that harsher punishment was the key to crime reduction. Cutting the supply of drugs was rated as the least important step to reduce crime.

Another poll by the Gallup organization asked people which drugs they wanted to see eliminated. Alcohol ranked first. But crack came in second. Twenty-two percent of the respondents considered it most dangerous. The additional substances of concern, in diminishing order, were other forms of cocaine, then heroin and marijuana.

Those who believe the best way to cut drug use is to cut the supply cite the steady drop in the supply of drugs during the first half of this century. The result

was a constant decline in the number of addicts, from over 1 million to fewer than 10,000. Then, in the years after World War II, the supply started to rise. So did the number of addicts.

One method of curbing supply is to strike at the source. This means discouraging the coca-growing countries from cultivating the plant. The second way is to seal our borders against smugglers of cocaine. And finally, method three targets the distribution system within the United States, to try to prevent dealers from operating here.

STRIKING AT THE SOURCE

Every American president promises to wage an all-out international war against drugs. Each seeks to convince producer countries to control the growth, production, and shipment of drugs. Our government has tried to help the governments of producing countries to clamp down on the drug growers and manufacturers within their borders.

But despite all these efforts, about 335,000 metric tons of coca were imported into the United States in 1991, according to the International Narcotics Control Strategy Report.

In 1986 President Ronald Reagan signed a $1.7 billion antidrug bill into law. The law attempted to cut back the influx of drugs coming into this country by automatically suspending half the foreign aid to every major drug producing and drug trafficking country for

Americans are arrested in Key West, Florida, for smuggling drugs by boat.

one year. When the country did not show significant progress in controlling the drug traffic, the suspended aid was directed elsewhere.

Cutting drug production abroad has proven difficult because so many foreign farmers make their living in the drug industry. An estimated one million farmers and laborers in Peru, Bolivia, and Colombia grow coca leaves and process and export coca products. As many as 60,000 Peruvian families depend on coca harvests for their livelihood. Five percent or more of the population of Bolivia is directly employed in the cocaine industry.

Colombia is a good example of a country that has tried to cut its supply of cocaine to the United States. The drug flow began in 1959, after a number of traffickers fled Cuba following the communist revolution and settled in Colombia. Here the Cuban exiles set up laboratories to process the coca leaves grown in Peru and Bolivia. And they set up distribution systems to get the processed drug to the United States, Canada, and Europe.

Now the former Cubans continue to process and distribute the drug in increased quantities. And they have also begun cultivating the coca plants in Colombia as well. Experts estimate that as many as 37,000 acres of coca are being farmed now in Colombia.

For much of the 1980s, the Medellin and Cali cartels in Colombia controlled up to 80 percent of the cocaine sent to the United States. Although at first the two cartels peacefully shared the U.S. market, a struggle for control of the New York market erupted in violence in 1988. The feud resulted in the deaths of at least twelve Colombians in New York City. The two groups informed on each other and enabled Colombian and U.S. government officials to successfully prosecute more Colombian drug dealers, weakening the power of the two cartels.

Every year since 1973, the U.S. government, has

given Colombia money and technical assistance to combat the drug trade in that country. In 1990, the U.S. government provided about $82 million for direct assistance to foreign drug control. Most of the money went to Latin American countries, with Colombia receiving the largest percentage of the funds. But this has not cut the supply greatly. Most government officials feel that cocaine production remains about the same.

Production dips that did occur in the 1980s were partly due to the 1984 assassination of Rodrigo Lara Bonilla, Colombia's minister of justice. Bonilla was one of the strongest foes of the illegal drug traffic. His murder by drug traders unleashed a powerful government reaction, leading to dozens of arrests, destruction of many acres of coca plants, and the closing of a number of cocaine-processing laboratories.

Coca fields are also plentiful in Peru, where over half the total coca production originated in 1990. Twelve percent of the U.S. government's 1990 drug control assistance budget went to shut down drug-related activities in Peru. The money was intended to be used to destroy coca plant fields and to convince Peruvian farmers to grow rice or cacao instead of coca.

But the police in Peru do not have the cooperation they need. Not only are they shot at by drug traffickers but by big farmers also. Then, leftist rebels, who are often supported with funds from the drug trade, join in the assaults. As one example, a 160-man special cocaine strike force was disbanded after nineteen of its members were killed.

Despite its best efforts, the U.S. government has not enjoyed much success in reducing worldwide production of the coca leaves that are essential to the production of crack. In fact, between 1987 and 1991, worldwide production of coca leaf rose from 291,000 to 337,000 metric tons.

OPERATION BLAST FURNACE

Bolivia, located next to Peru, is the poorest country in South America. Between 350,000 and 400,000 Bolivians are directly employed in the cocaine industry, and about 26 percent of total coca production comes from Bolivia. Most of the Bolivian crop is sent to Colombia for processing and distribution. But there is a growing movement for Bolivian drug traffickers—called the "Coca Nostra"—to do their own processing.

The U.S. government began sending assistance to Bolivia in 1972 to help cut the cocaine traffic. In August 1980 the program was suspended after several highranking Bolivian government officials were found to have links to cocaine production. It was resumed three years later when there was a change of government.

In July 1986 several giant U.S. Air Force transport planes landed in central Bolivia. From the planes came six Army Black Hawk helicopters and 160 pilots, communications experts, and ground support crews. The soldiers, who were armed with M-16 rifles, were under orders to fire only if fired on. This was the start of Operation Blast Furnace, the first American military operation to fight drugs on foreign soil.

The Americans were there at the invitation of Bolivian President Victor Paz Estenssor. The purpose was to help the Leopards, Bolivia's special antidrug police. The plan involved striking a blow at the Bolivian drug traffickers by raiding some thirty-five factories, landing strips, and warehouses. It was supposed to be a sixty-day operation.

Unfortunately there was a great deal of advance knowledge and publicity about Operation Blast Furnace. The drug traffickers and their equipment were gone long before the American helicopters landed the Leopards at the suspected sites. And because of poor intelligence, in some cases the Leopards charged with drawn guns into empty cattle barns.

Almost no traffickers were captured in Operation Blast Furnace. The biggest quarry was a seventeen-year-old boy who claimed that his only job was to wash the planes used to haul the cocaine. Precious few cocaine factories were found. The ones that were discovered proved to be little more than ramshackle collections of tents and huts.

Yet, both the American and Bolivian authorities claim that Operation Blast Furnace met its goals. "My government considers the operation a great success," said Bolivian ambassador Fernando Illanes. The knowledge that the Americans and the Bolivian Leopards were in the area, ready to pounce on any evidence of cocaine manufacture or transportation, he said, was enough to put a real dent in the drug's production.

A good number of people questioned the logic of Operation Blast Furnace. Why go after the factories? Why not destroy the thousands of acres of coca plants?

The reason is that raising coca is legal in Bolivia. Only making the coca into cocaine is against the law. And coca in Bolivia is a very important cash crop. It earns the country about $600 million a year. The harvest supports up to 400,000 *campesinos,* or peasant farmers, and their families.

In December 1985, the Bolivian government offered the *campesinos* over $100 per acre to grow other crops, such as citrus fruits. But there were no takers. A government drug official explained why: "*Campesinos* are rational economic individuals. There is no other crop that will provide the kind of income that coca provides." It is estimated that the peasants can earn up to $4,000 raising coca on the same acre of land.

Operation Blast Furnace hoped that closing the labs and factories would force down the price that the *campesinos* get for their coca leaves. Then it might become more profitable for them to grow another crop.

This did not happen. But the operation did succeed in disrupting the Bolivian economy. On July 30, 1986, Ambassador Illanos asked for a $100 million loan to make up for the revenue lost because of Operation Blast Furnace.

Four years later the U.S. government enjoyed slightly better success in its efforts to reduce the flow of coca out of Bolivia. The U.S. Department of State reports that about 14 percent of the estimated Bolivian crop of coca was successfully wiped out in 1990.

SEAL THE BORDERS

Soon after taking office in 1981, President Ronald Reagan declared a war on drug trafficking. The main battleground was to be our nation's borders.

Among his first actions was a push for amendments to the Posse Comitatus Act. This act prohibits military personnel from having police powers over civilians. It was originally passed right after the Civil War. The purpose was to calm the fear of Southerners that the U.S. Army might act as an occupying force. The 1981 amendments gave the government permission to use the armed services in the fight against drugs.

The following year, the Reagan administration put Vice President George Bush in charge of a newly established South Florida Task Force. This task force coordinated the activities of nine separate law-enforcement agencies: the U.S. Attorney's Office; the Drug Enforcement Administration (DEA); the Federal Bureau of Investigation (FBI); the Customs Service; the Bureau of Alcohol, Tobacco and Firearms; the Internal Revenue Service; the Coast Guard; the Border Patrol; and the U.S. Marshals. Its purpose is to seal the Florida coast—long a favorite route of entry for cocaine—against all drug smugglers.

In November 1982, after less than half a year of operation of the South Florida Task Force, President Reagan visited Florida. Surrounded by tons of confiscated cocaine, Reagan proclaimed the project a huge success. He called it "a brilliant example of working federalism."

The South Florida Task Force seized nearly $20 million in drugs, cash, and weapons from drug suppliers, dealers, and users in its first twelve months of operation. That was 50 percent more than was confiscated the year before. The U.S. Attorney in south Florida brought 664 drug cases to trial—an increase of 64 percent over the previous year. And many large shipments of drugs were prevented from entering the country.

Yet the drug trade kept growing. The drugs that are seized, experts believe, represent but a small fraction of the total volume of illegal drugs that are being smuggled into the United States.

Why is more cocaine entering the country than ever before?

Some say it is because the government has been *too* successful in stopping drugs at the border. Smugglers and dealers have switched to cocaine from other drugs for the greater profits. Marijuana, for example, is bulky and cheap. A ton of marijuana, about the size of an automobile, is worth only as much as a 2-pound (.9-kg) bag of cocaine. The more expensive cocaine is much smaller and therefore easier to handle and hide.

Cocaine smugglers get an A-plus for creativity. One smuggler who got caught had a half pound of cocaine surgically implanted under the skin of each of his thighs. Another smuggler had concealed the drug in a stuffed teddy bear. More than a ton of cocaine was once found wrapped in plastic packets inside drums of guava pulp, 496 pounds (225 kilograms) of cocaine were found packed in false-bottomed boxes labeled as toilet seats, and 2,400 pounds (1088.6 kilograms) of cocaine were found packaged in anchovy cans shipped from Argentina. Panamanian cocaine smugglers discovered a way to combine cocaine with vinyl to produce a material that can be used to make luggage and sneakers. The cocaine could be separated from the vinyl when the shipment reached its destination. Crack concealed in a box of Cheese Nips was once seized in a Greyhound bus station.

Others argue that trying to seal the borders is just not the best way to stop the spread of cocaine. Such efforts, though, are very popular with the legislators who decide on the funding for the war on drugs. Capturing a cocaine shipment is very dramatic and makes for an exciting item on the TV evening news. It is "cleaner" and "neater" than trying to catch the traffickers, distributors, and street dealers all around the country. And it is surely easier than trying to convince foreign countries to destroy the coca plants, one of their most profitable crops.

The 1986 antidrug law slightly improved the ability of the Customs Service and Coast Guard to stop the flow of drugs into the country. The law provided them with four high-tech E-2C radar planes, seven radar Aerostat balloons, and eight Blackhawk helicopters. In 1989, Congress enacted a law that designated the Department of Defense the lead agency for stopping the movement of illegal drugs by air and sea. However, Congress did not authorize the military to make arrests or conduct searches of civilians.

Pete, a "detector dog" working for the U.S. Cutoms Service, sniffs an airplane in search of illegal drugs.

Before the task force, Florida was the major entry area for South American cocaine. When agents secured those borders, the drug traffickers merely moved their operations. Some went west along the Gulf Coast to Alabama, Louisiana, and Texas. Others moved to entry points farther north.

The South Florida Task Force may have unknowingly led to an increase in cocaine smuggling in another way. Drawing a tight net around the Florida coast forced the smugglers to look for ways to cut their losses. One way is to divide the shipments among a number of small boats. This minimizes the losses. And it lets most of the shipments get through without trouble.

One thing is sure. No matter what the authorities do, cocaine imports keep increasing.

DISRUPTIONS TO DISTRIBUTION

The government also hopes to stop the drug trade by seizing the money that changes hands in illegal drug sales. One crack dealer interviewed by reporter Doublas Montero of the *Amsterdam News* estimated that he could take in a million dollars a year pushing crack on the street.

Billions and billions of dollars that are made in the drug trade are hidden from the view of the authorities in a process known as "laundering." The object of laundering is to convert "dirty" drug money into "clean," or legitimate, money. This is usually done by passing the drug money through a bank, often a foreign bank, a legitimate business, or a mob-run business that has a legitimate front.

Jim Bramble, a special agent with the DEA, once said, "From the point of view of combatting drug trafficking, the only way to put these people out of business is to remove the capital from the business. You

The U.S. Coast Guard confiscates illegal drugs found on boats.

can put them in jail for ten years and when they get out of jail if they still have that $40 million bank account in Switzerland or Panama or Grand Cayman, they go right back in business."

The United States has signed agreements with Switzerland and the Cayman Islands that enable it to obtain secret banking records of people involved in drug violation cases. The departments of Justice and State negotiated with Panama and the Bahamas, which also keep their banking records concealed, for similar treaties. These treaties do not, however, eliminate the difficulties in obtaining the information needed to prosecute money launderers. Some countries, for example, notify the subject of the investigation that the U.S. government has requested information, thus alerting the launderer of the need to move the illegal funds. Sometimes foreign banking laws give the owner of the funds the right to appeal the release of the information, which often blocks or delays the investigation. In 1990 the United States participated in three international conferences to curb drug-related money laundering.

The less-than-impressive results from Colombia, Peru, and Bolivia, combined with growing concerns about the flow of cocaine across the borders, are making Congress think about new ways to curb the spread of drugs. Widespread publicity about crack is making legislators reconsider policies that focus on cutting supply. The belief is growing that the best way to get at crack and other forms of cocaine is not to nibble away at suppliers but to discourage demand.

7
CUTTING DEMAND

"Smoke? Psst. Smoke?" whispers John, a skinny teenager, to people passing by. It is late Saturday night in Washington Heights, a neighborhood in upper New York City. Besides those just strolling along, a steady line of cars is slowly cruising back and forth. Every once in a while John raises his hand and makes believe he is cracking an imaginary whip in the air. John is one of the many crack dealers who can be found on street corners in American cities today.

An expensive, late-model car pulls up near the crack seller. Two young couples coming from a prom in New Jersey are inside. The driver, a tuxedo-clad young man about nineteen years old, jumps out and slips the seller two $100 bills. The street dealer takes the money, reaches into his jacket pocket, and pulls out a handful of small vials.

At that moment, two undercover cops who have been hiding in the shadows of a building dash out. Within seconds they have both the dealer and the customer in handcuffs. The cops tell the customer that they are also taking his car.

Both the dealer and buyer will go to trial. If convicted under federal law, the seller could receive up to thirty years in prison if this was not his first offense.

A billboard warning of crack's deadly potential

The buyer will be sentenced to five to twenty years in prison, depending on whether he has been previously convicted of possession of crack cocaine. After the trial, the car will either be sold or used by undercover officers.

Some time later, the nineteen-year-old whose car was seized was asked for his reactions. "I'm not happy about it," he said. "But I think it'll teach people a lesson. It certainly taught me one. I'm not going back to that scene."

STRICTER LAWS

Federal courts, and some state courts, rely on sentencing guidelines when punishing violators of drug laws. The guidelines for setting an appropriate sentence include consideration of the defendant's criminal history, the dangerousness of the drug, the amount of the drug involved, the ages of the parties involved in the drug transaction, and the location of the drug sale. Federal judges can sentence a first-time drug offender convicted of possessing any amount of any type of illegal drug to up to one year in prison and a fine of up to $1,000—with one exception. This exception applies to persons convicted of possessing certain drugs containing cocaine base, such as crack-cocaine.

Persons convicted of offenses involving crack-cocaine face much stiffer penalties under "mandatory minimum sentencing." Under this rule, a first-time offender, convicted of possessing five grams of crack-cocaine will be sentenced to a mandatory minimum of five years, and a maximum of twenty years in prison. A federal judge can only order a lesser sentence if the prosecutor determines that the defendant provided "substantial assistance" to the government in its prosecution of other drug offenders.

Those who favor mandatory minimum sentences believe that drug use and dealing will go down as the certainty of punishment goes up. Those opposed to mandatory minimum sentences point out that similar laws in effect in New York in the early 1970s did not stem illegal drug use. They also argue that the laws will result in prison overcrowding, tax the resources of the judicial system, and leave convicted drug addicts without the rehabilitation and treatment services they need.

Over the past decade, federal sentences for drug offenders have been increasing in severity. Between 1980 and 1989 the average sentence for a federal drug offender went up 59 percent. By 1989 drug offenders accounted for 49 percent of all federal prisoners; in 1980, only 27 percent of all federal prisoners were drug offenders.

Some experts believe that it takes more than fear of punishment to stop the habitual user. Addicts would sooner take a chance on a long prison term than give up crack. Also, some think that the ones who will get caught under the stricter laws will not necessarily be the heavy users but those who are simply not experienced enough to avoid detection.

There is also some concern that stricter penalties for crack use, possession, and sale disproportionately affects minorities. Blacks are arrested primarily for possession and dealing crack, while whites are arrested for powder cocaine. In July 1993, Federal Judge Lyle E. Strom of Omaha, Nebraska ruled that blacks convicted in crack cases received substantially—and illegally—longer prison sentences than

A drug raid at a crack house in Houston, Texas

whites, who are generally convicted in cases involving powder cocaine. The year before, Minnesota Judge Pamela Alexander also found a state law to be discriminatory because it penalized possession of crack more severely than it penalized possession of powdered cocaine. Drug prosecutors respond that anticrack laws are not racist but are intended to help black communities by getting crack off the streets.

Some feel that stricter law enforcement may unintentionally increase drug-related crime on the streets. The confiscation of crack or the capture of a drug trafficker surely makes less cocaine available for sale. But scarcity makes the price go up. And with higher cost, the abusers need more money. The result is more muggings and robberies by desperate abusers of the drug.

Several states are calling for special drug laws that will impact on crack and other drugs. One such law considers a person guilty of unlawfully dealing with a child if he or she allows the child to enter a place where drug activity is going on. Another makes it a crime to drive while under the influence of cocaine or another drug. And still other laws make it an offense for the driver to refuse to submit to a drug test.

In some areas, the police are enforcing little-used laws that forbid the sale of supplies and materials needed to prepare drugs. These laws are commonly referred to as "antidrug paraphernalia" laws. The Federal Government and the District of Columbia and every state except Alaska, have some type of law restricting the sale, import, and/or export of drug paraphernalia. Violation of the federal antidrug paraphernalia law is punishable by up to three years in jail and a $250,000 fine. Police officers have used the antidrug paraphernalia laws to raid stores that carry the equipment needed to smoke crack, such as pipes.

In recent years some drug offenders who are convicted of possessing small amounts of drugs, or of nonviolent drug-related offenses, are sentenced to "intermediate sanctions." Intermediate sanctions fall somewhere between incarceration in prison and traditional probation. One example of an intermediate sanction is the shock incarceration program. Drug offenders sentenced to a shock incarceration program are confined for up to six months in a military-style boot camp where they must confront physical and mental challenges that are designed to boost their self-esteem and self-control. Another example of an intermediate sanction is intensively supervised probation, or ISP. With ISP the offender is closely monitored for criminal activity and must often undergo drug treatment, drug testing, community service, and/or electronic monitoring as a condition of probation. Day Reporting Centers are also used in connection with intermediate sanctions. Offenders are often required to attend the Day Reporting Centers on a regular and frequent basis to receive job training, counseling, education, recreation, and drug testing.

In some areas, undercover agents stake out places where crack is being sold. From their hiding places, they look out for car drivers who come to the area for the drug. As soon as a sale is made, they arrest the buyer and seller. What's more, they also seize the automobile.

The police act under a federal law that allows authorities to impound any vehicle used in a drug deal. The law was intended to confiscate the cars, boats, and airplanes of drug traffickers. Now it is being used to take away the cars of drug consumers. In 1990 the Federal Drug Enforcement Agency seized assets worth more than $364 million, including 5,674 cars valued at over $60 million, 187 ships valued at over

$16 million, and 51 airplanes worth more than $25 million.

DECRIMINALIZATION

The best way to cut the demand for cocaine and crack, some say, is to remove criminal penalties from its sale or use. Pass laws that would regulate drug production and consumption. Treat crack like alcohol, so that fewer people would make money from its illegal sale.

In the *Wisconsin Law Review,* Steven Wisotsky wrote an article called "Exposing the War on Cocaine: The Futility and Destructiveness of Prohibition." Here he gave the best-known argument for decriminalization: The heavy users, who consume most of the cocaine, will do anything to get their fix. Therefore, make it available at a reasonable price so they will not have to rob innocent people to buy the stuff.

According to Wisotsky, the economics of cocaine contributes to its spread. One gram of chemically pure cocaine prepared by a legal drug manufacturer costs less than $2. But the same gram prepared in an illegal laboratory and cut with adulterants will fetch up to $150 on the street. The huge profits of illegal cocaine and crack attract underworld characters to the drug trade. Consumers of illegal drugs spent $18 billion for cocaine in 1990, according to the Office of National Drug Control Policy. With such big money comes crime, violence, corruption, tax evasion, and destruction of moral and ethical values.

Dr. Berger would provide crack free at government clinics and at the same time help abusers to break the habit. With this approach, he says, "the addict will be regarded for what he is—a sick person. We cannot cure a complicated social, economic, and medical disease with a policeman's billy."

The immense profits from cocaine have made millionaires of many top drug traffickers in South America and the Caribbean islands. Their tremendous wealth has brought them great power. In some cases it has even allowed them to influence the government and install regimes that are sympathetic to their drug business.

Back at home, Wisotsky worries that the civil rights of Americans may be violated in the attempt to stamp out drugs. Police may begin doing wiretaps without the proper authority. Illegal searches and seizures may become rampant. Involuntary drug tests or confiscation of property are already being challenged in the courts. Do we not lose more than we gain if we cut demand for drugs but weaken some of our civil rights in the process?

Despite presenting some convincing arguments for decriminalization, Wisotsky himself says: "It has no chance. Society isn't ready for it." Most Americans, and their elected officials, do not approve of the decriminalization of drugs. Eighty percent of those who responded to a 1990 Gallup poll thought it would be a "bad idea" to legalize, tax, and regulate cocaine like alcohol and tobacco. Most people reported believing that drug use in the public schools would increase if drugs are legalized, as would the number of drug addicts and drug overdoses. In response to public opinion, many legislators are moving in quite the opposite direction—toward even more stringent laws and increased enforcement.

There are also legal obstacles to decriminalization. No state can decriminalize crack because federal law prohibits its use, and federal law supersedes state law. On the next level, the federal government cannot legalize crack because the United States signed the United Nations Single Convention on Narcotic Drugs. The law forbids any nonmedical use of cocaine or other drug of abuse. This international agreement supersedes any single nation's laws. The decriminalization of crack would go against the United States' obligations as a signer of the Convention.

Britain has a long history of drug decriminalization. Since the 1920s, an addict could obtain a prescription for legal heroin. This system worked well while the number of addicts remained low.

But around 1960, when there was a big increase in the number of users, the system began breaking down. People who had prescriptions for the drug began selling their heroin to others. Some addicts who felt that they were not getting enough legally also started buying and trading on the black market. Because of its many problems, the heroin-by-prescription plan has by now been almost completely abandoned in Britain.

Before cocaine and crack can be decriminalized some important questions must be answered: What should be the lowest age for people to be able to buy crack? Should it be eighteen? Twenty-one? The voting age? The drinking age? If teenagers can't buy crack, won't that create an illegal underworld to supply them with drugs? Which forms of cocaine should be made available to the public? Will the law be the same for each type?

Illegal dealers, it is argued, will always be able to provide a wider range of choices to more people than any government-approved methods of distribution. And finally, what of the principles involved? There is understandable concern that legalizing drug use will create a society of drug-crazed zombies.

DRUG TESTING

The question of drug testing became an issue of considerable public debate in the summer of 1986. A 1989 Gallup poll reported that Americans were pretty evenly split on the issue of mandatory blood testing. But a clear majority, over 90 percent, felt that drug testing was a good idea for airline pilots, transportation workers, and truck drivers. Between 80 and 90 percent of those surveyed felt that drug testing was a good idea for health care, construction, and utility workers. Only 61 percent felt that office workers should be tested. Many people who oppose drug testing do so on civil rights grounds; they believe mandatory drug testing violates workers' rights of privacy.

In July 1986 a device for drug testing at home first became available. The kit, called Aware, was put out by American Drug Screens, Inc., of Dallas, Texas. For under $30 anyone, such as a parent, could go to a drugstore and buy Aware. The parents would then get a urine sample from their son or daughter, mail it to the lab, and within two weeks receive a report on whether their child has been doing crack.

Those in favor of home testing think the kits give youngsters an excuse to refuse drugs by saying that their parents are testing them and they're afraid of getting caught. Positive results, they believe, encourage families to seek help.

Others oppose the home use of testing kits. They feel that testing is best left to the professionals. Kids who are abusing crack might refuse to provide a specimen, get someone else to fill the bottle, or add chemicals that will throw off the test results.

The U.S. Supreme Court in 1989 upheld drug testing of public employees even when there is no suspicion of drug use or impairment, at least when public safety is involved. There is mandatory drug testing for members of the armed forces and for employees of such agencies as the Federal Bureau of Investigation, Postal Service, Drug Enforcement Administration, Federal Aviation Administration, and Immigration and Naturalization Service.

Drug testing in the military has had good results.

In 1980, experts estimated that about 28 percent of all military personnel was doing some sort of drugs. After the Department of Defense started a mandatory drug-testing program, by 1988 the number of drug users went down to about 5 percent. Similarly, within the first six months of testing troops returning from Vietnam, the Department of Defense found the rate of positive test results drop from 5 percent to under 2 percent.

There are, of course, occasions when people who never used drugs in their life get positive test results. For example, an employee of the New York City Transit Authority who never went near crack but was taking diet pills tested positive. Three-fourths of a football team, all drug-free, failed the test because of a painkiller they were taking.

In recent years, scientists have been experimenting with the use of hair and bodily fluids, such as tears and perspiration, for drug testing. Many people consider these methods preferable for detecting drug abuse because these methods are less invasive than collecting blood samples. These tests also detect drug use over a longer period of time. While cocaine is evident in urine for only two or three days after use, hair analysis can reveal week-long or month-long patterns of drug use. These new methods are not yet as useful and accurate as blood and urine drug tests. Additional research on drug testing is required.

There are several legal and constitutional arguments against drug testing. The primary concern is each individual's right to privacy.

Urine samples at a lab in Pennsylvania waiting to be tested for traces of illegal drugs

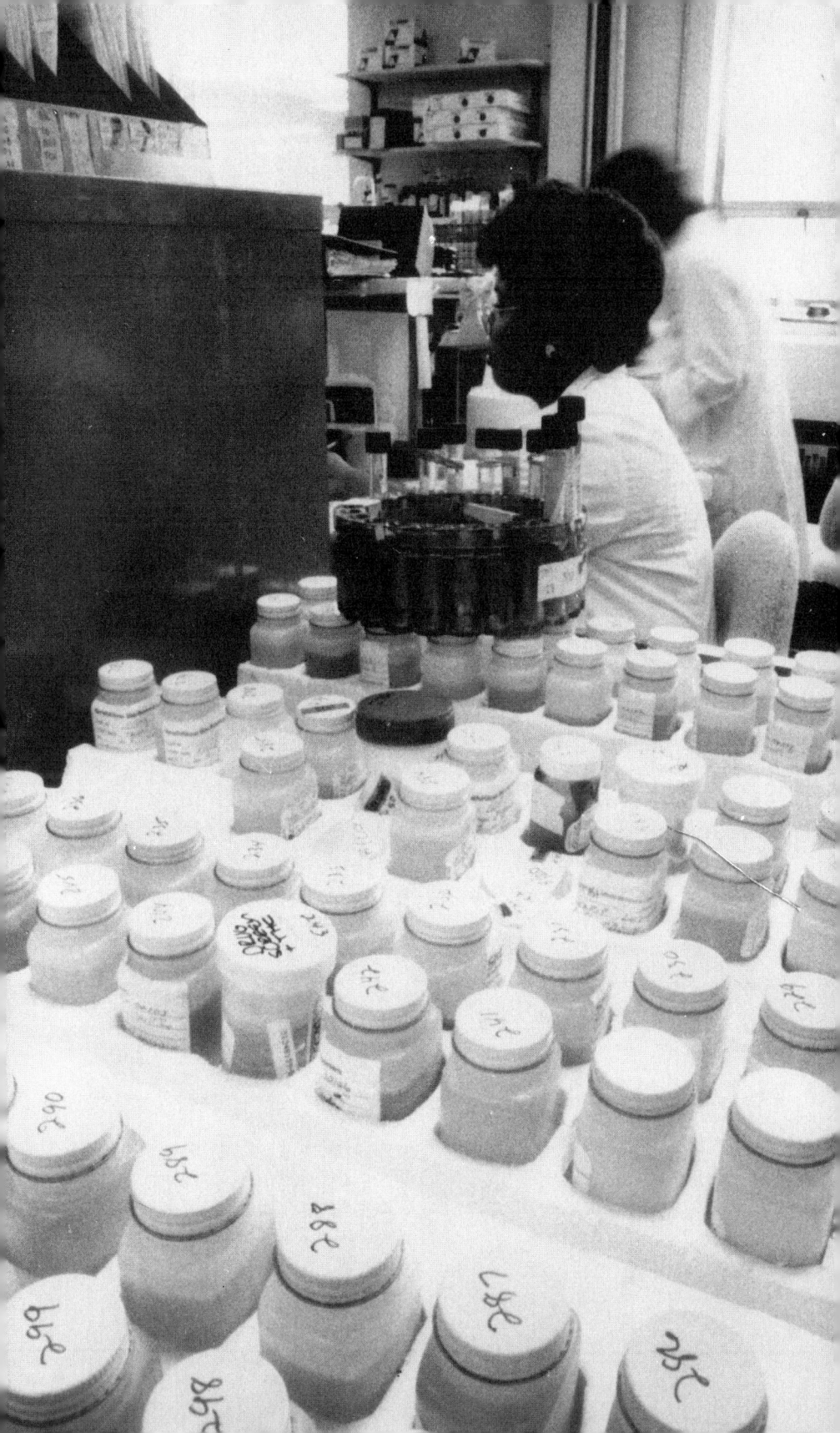

Does an employer have the right to test a worker for drugs if there is no evidence that drugs are affecting the worker's performance on the job? Someone can go to a party on Saturday night, smoke crack, and have some small trace found in his urine on Monday morning. But isn't that different from someone who smokes crack on the job and messes up his work?

Most employers say they are only interested in whether crack, or any other drug, is interfering with the worker's performance on the job. But with widespread mandatory tests, the occasional weekend smoker and the daily abuser would be found equally guilty.

There are also some economic objections to drug testing. A urine test for drugs costs between $15 and $250, depending on the level of accuracy required. Just one test of all workers in America would cost between $1 billion and $27 billion. Even if there were only random tests of a few workers from time to time, the numbers and cost would still be high. Who would pay for these tests?

Also, if the object of drug testing is not to punish (or fire) the workers, but to help them conquer the addiction, who will pay the thousands of dollars necessary to treat those who test positive?

Experts agree that treatment programs are already short billions of dollars needed for adequate treatment of those presently enrolled in those programs. Using testing to stop or discourage drug use is a very costly solution, and one that may be easily abused.

EDUCATION

The widespread outrage over crack suggests a big shift in public attitudes. Longer jail sentences and drug testing are two favorite solutions being offered by government officials. But almost everyone agrees that the best way to fight drugs is through education, prevention, and treatment. If those methods succeed, the question of new laws and drug testing becomes irrelevant.

While most of the government's drug control efforts during the first half of the 1980s were aimed at reducing the supply of drugs, by the late 1980s the focus was shifting to reducing the demand for drugs. The Anti-Drug Abuse Act of 1986 authorized expanded drug treatment programs and created the Office for Substance Abuse Prevention. The 1988 Anti-Drug Abuse Act also increased treatment and prevention efforts in an attempt to reduce the demand for drugs. The 1989 National Drug Control Strategy urged an evaluation of different drug treatment programs and approaches to find what worked best. The Crime Control Act of 1990 expanded drug education programs in the public schools.

The Federal government's 1986 drug law provided an additional $200 million to the Department of Education for special drug prevention and education programs. In 1991 the Department of Education distributed $497.7 million of federal funds for drug education and prevention programs. Many complain that this still isn't enough money to educate schoolchildren to the dangers of drugs.

The Rand Corporation, a think tank, has studied approaches to drug prevention through education. According to its report, the method should resemble the one used to convince adolescents not to smoke. First, focus on the immediate effects rather than long-term health perils. In the antismoking campaign this meant stressing such factors as bad breath and discolored teeth more than the increased danger of lung cancer in the future. Then, focus on prevention rather than punishment. And finally, allowing for some teenage

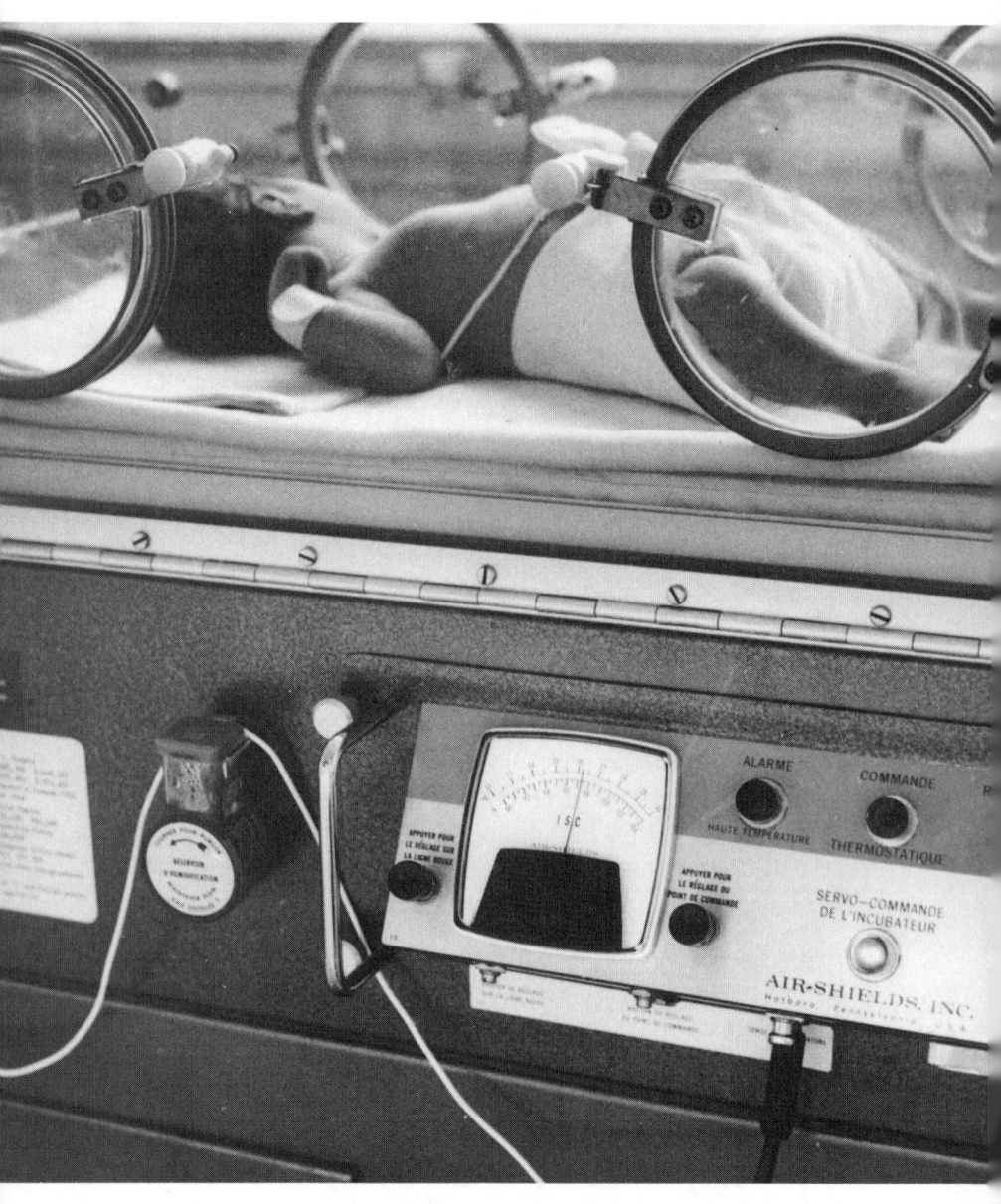
Crack babies, infants of mothers who smoked crack while pregnant, often suffer many disabilities.

experimentation, provide objective, accurate information about illegal drugs.

Antidrug education programs take many forms. The Department of Education, for example, printed 15 million copies of a handbook for parents on raising drug-free children, and distributed 5,000 handbooks for a drug-free campus to college presidents. The federal Office of Substance Abuse Prevention (OSAP) has published 4 million coloring books with antidrug themes for children, and produced an action video called "Wally Bear & the NO Gang," which encourages children to refuse drugs. The Department of Justice, together with the private advertising industry, has sponsored the McGruff Crime Dog "Users are Losers" antidrug campaign.

Will education work in the face of today's crack epidemic? During Prohibition there was a nationwide effort to educate everyone, young and old, on the dangers of alcohol. Yet, there is no evidence that this curbed the desire for alcohol to any extent.

Many drug prevention and treatment programs are currently available in schools, community groups, and treatment centers in every state and large city across the country. A number of large corporations, including General Motors, Union Pacific, U.S. Tobacco, Kidder Peabody, and Alcoa, have set up programs to counsel and treat employees with drug problems. And the various professional sports leagues are starting screening programs to discover and help athletes on drugs.

CHILD ABUSE CHARGES

One of the most unfortunate consequences of the crack epidemic has been crack use by pregnant women. A pregnant woman who uses crack exposes her fetus to the drug.

In an effort to discourage drug use by pregnant

women, nineteen states have passed laws that allow child abuse charges to be filed against any woman who gives birth to a baby who is born with illegal drugs in his or her bloodstream. In some cases, babies who have been exposed to crack in the womb are taken away from their mothers. In other cases, felony drug charges are brought against the drug-addicted mother.

The issue of punishing women who expose the fetuses they are carrying to drugs came to the fore in the late 1980s and early 1990s in two cases. One case involved Kimberly Ann Hardy, who smoked crack the night before she gave birth to a son in August 1989. The other case involved Lynn Bremer, who snorted cocaine forty hours before giving birth to her daughter in April 1990. In both cases, charges were pressed against the mothers for delivering drugs to their infants.

Critics of this use of the child abuse laws charge that babies who are removed from their mother's care often end up in worse shape than those who are left at home with a drug-addicted mother. Children who become wards of the state are commonly left for months in the hospital (so-called "boarder babies"). The long-term effect on the child of this period of institutionalization and neglect can be lifelong emotional and physical problems. When they get older, these children are often placed in a series of foster homes. Their lives lack stability and security. Civil rights advocates and feminists also charge that prosecuting a woman for what she does during her pregnancy violates the woman's constitutional right to privacy.

Possibly the best use of child abuse laws is as a threat in order to encourage drug-addicted mothers to receive treatment for their addiction. Several successful drug rehabilitation programs combine treatment services for the mother with caregiving services for the child. Mothers who participate in the program are motivated to complete their treatment under the threat of being charged with child abuse if they drop out of the program.

COMPULSORY TREATMENT

Dr. Mark Gold and many others support the idea of cutting demand by committing cocaine addicts to treatment centers. He feels that this should be done on a compulsory basis, whether or not the person wants to be committed. We know that people can be placed involuntarily in mental hospitals if considered a threat to themselves or others. Alcoholics, too, are institutionalized for treatment. Now Dr. Gold thinks this idea should be extended to cocaine users, as an alternative to prison.

Compulsory treatment of cocaine addicts is completely legal. In the famous 1962 decision of *Robinson v. California,* the U.S. Supreme Court ruled that drug addiction is not a crime. And within that same decision the court declared that compulsory treatment for addicts is legal because it is in the best interest of the state.

Such a policy will probably encourage treatment. The wife of a crack-smoking husband, for example, might be reluctant to have him arrested, even though his habit might be destroying the family. But perhaps she will be willing to have him committed to a treatment center to help rid him of the crack habit.

Experts estimate that the number of people who need drug treatment is three or four times the number of people who receive drug treatment. In real numbers, this means that only about one-third of the 2.5 million Americans who clearly need drug treatment, and the 3 million additional Americans who probably need treatment, are being treated for drug abuse, ac-

Demonstrators protest against crack in New York City in October 1986, hoping to encourage the federal government to spend more money on the war against drugs.

cording to a recent National Drug and Alcohol Treatment Unit Survey.

Involuntary commitment strikes some with horror. It conjures up visions of a dictatorship, where people who criticize the government are put away in mental hospitals. The freedom to reject treatment is a basic civil liberty.

However, others counter, cocaine destroys the family, the community, and the workplace. Treating cocaine addicts enhances civil liberties all around. The English philosopher John Stuart Mill said: "The only purposes for which power can be rightfully exercised over any member of a civilized community, against his will, is to prevent harm to others."

CARE AND TREATMENT

"Hotline. Can I help you?"

"Yeah. My name is Sue. I'm fifteen years old. I've smoked crack three times over the last week."

"OK, go on."

"Well, now I'm getting scared. All the time I keep thinking of my next fix. I really dig the rush. But I'm afraid it's getting out of control. I want out. What can I do?"

"I can help you. I'll give you the name of a drug treatment center near where you live."

"Do I have to go into a hospital?"

"I don't think so. But I'm no doctor. The people at the drug treatment center will be able to give you the information. I can't."

"OK. I guess I'll give it a try."

"Great. Where do you live?"

"Houston, Texas."

"Do you have a pencil? Here's the phone number. . . . Give them a call and set up an appointment. It won't cost you anything—and it may save your life."

"Gee, thanks a lot. Wish me luck."

Sue's call is one of thousands that are made every day to local and national cocaine hotlines all around the country. Many of the callers are on crack and want help. They ask for places to go where they can receive care and treatment.

President Clinton, during his 1992 campaign for the presidency, advocated drug treatment on demand. At the time he criticized President Bush for "locking up addicts instead of treating them." He also acknowledged that punishing drug addicts was more popular among voters than treating them: "Emphasizing treatment may not satisfy people fed up with being preyed upon, but a president should speak straight even if what he advocates isn't popular." In his 1993 Interim National Drug Control Strategy Report, President Clinton strongly endorsed expanded drug treatment.

Critics of President Clinton's drug policy charge that, since taking office, the president has backed down on his pledge to promote drug treatment. He has not shifted federal antidrug dollars away from law enforcement and into drug treatment, as promised. As of the beginning of 1994, twice as many of the 13.1 billion federal antidrug dollars went to law enforcement as to drug treatment. The president is accused by his critics of giving in to public pressure to appear tough on crime, since few drug addicts are registered voters.

A proposed federal crime bill would allocate substantial funds to drug treatment. One version of the bill would provide almost every federal prisoner, and about half of state inmates, with intensive drug treatment by 1998.

In the United States there are presently about 12,000 long-term residential drug treatment beds. With at least 2 million Americans addicted to drugs, this is a mere drop in the bucket.

DETOXIFICATION

There is only one way to treat an addiction to crack. That way is to enter a drug treatment program in a hospital or other center. Certain programs are for outpatients. The patient goes to a center for therapy but continues to live at home and goes about most of his or her regular activities. Others sign themselves into live-in, residential programs, where they stay for as long as a year.

The choice of treatment usually depends on the severity of the addiction. In general, the earlier someone on crack goes for help, the easier and better are the chances for a successful outcome.

The purpose of residential treatment is to separate users from the environment in which they have been buying and using drugs. Such programs also provide intensive counseling and therapy to treat the basic causes that led to drug taking in the first place.

The first part of any drug-treatment program is detoxification, which literally means to rid the body of poisons or the effects of poisons. The process usually consists of three main steps:

First, get the person completely off the drug as soon as possible.

Second, relieve both the physical and psychological distress of the withdrawal process.

Third, achieve and maintain abstinence, or a drug-free life.

GETTING OFF CRACK

Take the case of Jimmy, eighteen, a serious abuser of crack. One day Jimmy bought some crack just before driving downtown. He broke up the rock in one vial, sprinkled the bits in a marijuana joint, and lit up. After inhaling deeply, he got into his car, stepped on the gas, and drove down the highway.

That's all that Jimmy can remember. When he came to, he was in the emergency room of a Los Angeles hospital. The doctor told him that he had been in a serious automobile accident. The car was completely demolished, and he had knocked over a telephone pole. But by some miracle he had survived with nothing worse than bruises and cuts all over his body. They said he would have to stay in the hospital overnight for observation.

The next morning, the doctor and Jimmy's parents came to his bedside. They told him that they were aware that he was on cocaine and that they were really afraid that he would kill himself. After a while, he agreed to be signed into the hospital to be treated for his addiction.

While his parents took care of the paperwork, a nurse took Jimmy to the cocaine unit of the hospital. Part of him wanted to run, to get away. But part of him knew he had to stay, to see this thing through.

The first five days were probably the most difficult Jimmy had ever lived through. He became extremely depressed and withdrawn. He slept up to eighteen hours a day. When he was awake, all he could think about was crack. In vivid detail, he would recall the taste of the crack fumes, the searing sensation in his lungs, and the energy surge he got as the drug reached his brain.

The hospital made sure that Jimmy stayed completely free of drugs in those early days of treatment. When he first came into the unit he was searched for vials that he might have smuggled in. Neither visitors nor mail were allowed, to prevent the drug from reaching Jimmy from the outside. And the nurses took frequent urine and blood samples as a further check for cocaine in his body.

From the start, a psychiatrist saw Jimmy daily. Her primary goal at this stage was to help Jimmy accept treatment. She let him understand that detoxification, which lasts about a week, is extremely hard to handle. Even when he became irritable and turned violent, he would get a lot of understanding from the staff. Everyone in the unit was used to the symptoms of withdrawal from crack and would help him in many ways.

PSYCHOLOGICAL TREATMENT

Following detoxification, patients like Jimmy begin a program of treatment that involves a team of therapists. They also join groups of other patients who are at various stages in their treatment. Being able to talk together and to hear one another's stories makes each person feel less alone and afraid.

The therapists also bring the family into the treatment process. In family therapy sessions, the members explore the situations that have led to drug taking in the first place. The patient and parents talk freely to each other about their problems—some for the first time in years. Seated next to each other, they explore relationships and look at things in the home that aroused anxiety and possibly triggered the use of drugs.

Part of the treatment has to do with becoming educated about crack. Patients learn how the drug affects the body, the process of addiction, and what it takes to avoid becoming hooked once again. Through films, talks, and readings, they begin to see how dangerous its effects are. This part of the program may be run like a regular school, with lessons to study and tests on the material.

Another approach is learning to say no to drugs. In treatment, the patients practice refusing cocaine in various staged situations. Someone may act the part of a drug dealer offering a smoke and calling the person "chicken" for not taking the drug, for example.

The patients then try out various ways of turning down the dealer.

Before discharge, some patients are asked to sign a contract with the hospital. In it, they agree to participate in an aftercare program that could last for up to a year. They promise to attend meetings at the hospital and take frequent drug tests to insure a drug-free life. If needed, members of the patient's family will meet with the therapist to smoothe over any rough spots. And finally, if the patient violates any of the provisions, he or she agrees to accept another period of hospitalization.

Some drug clinics in Colorado are now experimenting with a novel approach. Before starting to treat a professional—doctor, lawyer, pilot, nurse, accountant—they ask the person to write and sign a letter to the government office that issues their professional licenses. The letter states, "I have been abusing crack and I have entered treatment. I have, however, failed and cannot remain drug-free. Therefore, I am asking that my license to practice be revoked."

The letter is given to the therapist at the beginning of treatment. If at any time during the period of treatment the patient is found to be taking drugs, the therapist may mail the letter. The early results seem to show that the letter is helpful in therapy.

Counselors who specialize in the treatment of drug addiction see new hope in the use of psychological means to treat crack addiction. Dr. Richard Rawson, executive director of the Matrix drug treatment program in Los Angeles, believes that crack addiction is easier to overcome than other addictions, such as alcohol, heroin, or nicotine, because the effects of cocaine withdrawal are largely psychological. The Matrix program, which uses psychological counseling, enjoys a 70 percent success rate among middle-class crack addicts. The success rate among inner-city addicts is slightly lower.

ACHIEVING A DRUG-FREE LIFE

By avoiding contact with drug dealers and users, many former substance abusers manage to steer clear of any temptation to buy cocaine. When people start using drugs in their presence, they get up and leave the room. They refuse to help others obtain drugs; nor do they touch or handle drugs themselves. The best advice any counselor can give is this: Stay away from any places or situations where drugs might be available.

Many former addicts join Cocaine Anonymous (CA). This is a self-help organization modeled on the older Alcoholics Anonymous. It is made up of former abusers of the drug, as well as persons trying to break themselves of a cocaine habit. The group holds regular meetings in which members relate their experiences—the successes and the failures—in an attempt to work out their problems.

Abstinence from drugs usually goes along with a whole lifestyle change. Often the change involves getting plenty of stimulants—the natural kind, such as running and swimming.

Crack addiction can be treated, but it cannot be cured. No one is ever permanently free of the drug. "We look on cocaine addiction as a lifelong illness," said one counselor.

Patients can backslide and return to their old ways at any time. Sometimes ex-addicts get tired of the meetings, the urine tests, and the sessions with their therapist. But as most everyone knows, the program works. And it is the only known way to stay off crack.

Recovered patients say that they never felt better or stronger in their life. Breaking free of crack may be the most difficult thing people can do for themselves; but it is also the best.

*The children of drug abusers are also victims.
Group counseling is sometimes provided for them.*

CHEMICAL TREATMENTS

Residential treatment for heavy users is a long, difficult, expensive process. The costs may run over $500 a day! The search is on, therefore, for other courses of action.

One line of study seeks to find a so-called cocaine blocker. This is a chemical that stems the effects of the drug. The person in treatment would get no charge from smoking crack. Eventually, the loss of the high would lead the patient to stop using the substance.

Lithium is a chemical that may be able to block the euphoria produced by cocaine. Without the sought-after euphoria, patients may cease taking the drug. But they may also cease taking lithium, studies show. Until now, lithium seems to be most successful in treating cocaine abusers with certain mental disorders that normally respond to lithium. It is still not known whether the drug will prove useful for most cocaine abusers.

The drugs used in the treatment of depression, called antidepressants, are moderately successful for treating cocaine abuse chemically. First, they relieve the underlying depression that often accompanies cocaine abuse. In addition to blocking the cocaine's euphoric effects, the antidepressants may also reverse the neurochemical changes produced by cocaine.

Doctors at the Fair Oaks Hospital in Summit, New Jersey, have been looking for a drug to end the craving of addicts and break their habit. They operate on the theory that a lack of the brain chemical dopamine leads heavy users to crave cocaine. Therefore, in one study, they gave forty heavy users a prescription drug, bromocriptine, which imitates somewhat the work of dopamine in the brain. After taking the bromocriptine the users reported much less craving from the drug, along with a drop in the usual withdrawal symptoms. In a separate study on laboratory animals, doctors found that bromocriptine is not habit forming.

Cocaine-replacement drugs provide reactions similar to that from cocaine but without cocaine's bad side effects or risks of breaking the law. Several researchers are studying the idea of changing alcohol in some way to fill the bill. Alcohol, in small quantities, helps people relax and get rid of anxieties. But alcohol can also be addictive and harmful to the drinker's health. So the scientists are trying to come up with a "safe" alcohol.

Other studies are looking at different, nonalcoholic substances as substitutes for cocaine. A group did find that lidocaine, a legal local anesthetic, fooled some cocaine users into thinking they were getting cocaine. But thus far, no good, safe replacement for cocaine has been found.

Some people question the value of simply substituting one drug for another. But so-called replacement drugs, it is argued, may have several advantages. Since the patient gets the drug from a physician, the dosage is controlled. Also, the risky ties with dealers and cocaine abusers are broken.

It may take a long time before a real cure for crack addiction is found. Meanwhile, the need for more and better treatment programs keeps growing. The main problems are those of space and money.

ACUPUNCTURE

Acupuncture is a novel approach to controlling crack addiction. An acupuncturist pierces the skin with small needles in a number of strategic locations on the patient's body. For years, acupuncture has been used to cure a range of ailments, from headaches to footaches, but it is still new in the treatment of drug addiction.

Several hospitals in New York City use acupuncture therapy to treat patients who are addicted to crack. They report that acupuncture controls the patient's desire to take another dose of crack.

TREATMENT ON DEMAND

Drug treatment programs in American cities report that they are filled to capacity. The problem of giving treatment on demand for crack addiction can be solved if neighborhoods stop resisting the building of treatment centers in their areas. Also, the federal government will have to commit itself to building and funding more treatment centers all around the country.

The situation is critical. Many of the callers to the National Cocaine Hotline, 800-COCAINE, or the Cocaine Helpline, a hotline run by the National Institute on Drug Abuse, 800-662-HELP, are desperate for help. But many of the programs are completely full and have long waiting lists. Others are just too expensive for the average person to afford. All too often the abuser seeking to break the habit is sent right back to the street with no chance for help.

What our country needs is a *real* war on crack and the other drugs that are crippling it. This war has to be fought on many fronts: education—to inform everyone about crack and what it can do to human beings; supply—to cut down on the amount of drugs flowing into this country and through the streets of our cities; and demand—to cut down on the huge quantities of drugs used by people of all ages and backgrounds, but especially the young.

A 1990 Gallup poll indicated that many people—

The Daytop drug rehabilitation program provides job training, as drug use and unemployment are often linked.

40 percent—believe that teaching youngsters about the dangers of drugs is the best approach to the drug problem. Working with foreign governments to stop the export of drugs to the United States came in second at 28 percent, and arresting drug sellers was third at 19 percent. Another poll conducted the same year by the Associated Press and Media General found 57 percent of Americans surveyed favored treating drug users over punishing them.

Elected officials, all the way from the president through Congress and many state and local government officials, have pledged themselves to wage such a war. They seem to understand that drugs threaten our future as a nation and that it will take forceful, sensible, and compassionate steps to end this scourge on the land.

GLOSSARY

Abstinence. The state of being free of drug use.

Acquired Immune Deficiency Syndrome (AIDS). A disease that interferes with the body's ability to fight off infection.

Active ingredient. The chemical in a plant that produces mind-altering or toxic effects.

Addict. A person who habitually uses drugs and is physically or psychologically dependent on them.

Addiction. A chronic, compulsive, or uncontrollable urge to use drugs despite serious side effects and extreme disruption of one's relationships and values.

Adulterants. Different substances added to the cocaine that make it less pure.

Agitation. Excessive restlessness, such as hand-wringing, fidgeting, and other forms of constant motor activity; one of the major symptoms of nonfatal drug overdose.

AIDS. See Acquired Immune Deficiency Syndrome.

Alkaloids. Chemicals known as bases, containing nitrogen, carbon, oxygen, and hydrogen.

Amphetamines. Drugs that stimulate the central nervous system, giving users the same sort of high as reported from cocaine, though not as powerful.

Angel dust. See PCP.
Antidepressants. Drugs used in the treatment of depression; they relieve the underlying depression that often accompanies cocaine abuse.
Base houses. Places where crack is sold and smoked.
Binges. Periods of uncontrolled and continuous drug use.
Bromocriptine. A prescription drug that somewhat imitates the effects of dopamine in the brain.
Coca. The plant or leaves from which cocaine is made.
Cocaine. A substance refined from the leaves of the coca plant that is a short-acting but powerful stimulant.
Cocaine Anonymous. A self-help group for abusers of cocaine modeled on Alcoholics Anonymous.
Cocaine blocker. A drug that stems the effects of cocaine.
Cocaine bugs. A feeling that cocaine users get of insects crawling on or under the skin.
Cocaine hydrochloride. Another name for powder cocaine.
Cocaine sulfate. See Coca paste.
Coca paste. A mash consisting of coca leaves with sulfuric acid and kerosene added.
Coke. A slang term for cocaine.
Coma. A state of unconsciousness from which the patient cannot be aroused.
Convulsions. Intense involuntary muscular contractions, which may follow crack abuse.
Crack. A very pure form of cocaine that is smoked.
Crack houses. See Base houses.
Crashing. The tiredness, irritability, and depression that occur after the effects of a drug begin to wear off.

Craving. A term implying both physical and psychological dependence; the user's "desire" or "need" to continue using a drug.

Dealing. The peddling or selling of drugs; the seller is called a dealer.

Delusion. A belief that exists in spite of reason, evidence, or facts to the contrary.

Depressant. Any drug that depresses the central nervous system, resulting in sedation and a decrease in bodily activity.

Depression. A mood characterized by feelings of inadequacy, lowered activity, and pessimism about the future.

Detoxification. Ridding the body of drugs or the effects of drugs through withdrawal and promoting recovery.

Dopamine. Chemical messengers in the brain that are thought to be associated with pleasurable feelings, alertness, and control of body movements.

Drug. Any substance, natural or artificial, that by its chemical nature alters structure or function in living organisms.

Drug abuse. A general term that describes the use of any substance prohibited by the law and that adversely affects a person's health and welfare.

Drug education. Any program designed to provide information on the use of drugs and to change people's attitudes and behavior regarding drugs.

Drug lords. The operators of small cocaine-manufacturing laboratories.

Dysphoria. A state of low energy, depression, anxiety, and restlessness, often accompanied by a noticeable lack of emotion.

Ether. A highly volatile and highly flammable liquid used in the manufacture of the form of cocaine known as freebase.

Euphoria. A state of extreme well-being and optimism often accompanied by heightened motor activity.

Family therapy. Treatment of more than one member of a family in the same session.

Flash. See Rush.

Freebase. A form of cocaine in which the hydrochloride is separated, or freed, from the other chemicals in the cocaine powder.

Group therapy. The technique of treating patients in groups instead of individually, emphasizing the fact that their problems are not unique.

Hallucinations. Perceptions of sounds and sights that do not really exist but arise from within the person.

Heroin. A highly addictive narcotic drug that is obtained from morphine.

High. The euphoria or exhilaration that the user feels while a drug is in effect.

Hits. Smokes of crack.

Hooked. Slang for becoming dependent on or addicted to a drug.

Hotline. A direct communications line, usually the telephone, for use in a crisis.

Hustling. Nonviolent means of making money illegally, such as theft, prostitution, and drug selling.

Injection. Taking a drug by forcing it in liquid form into some part of the body, usually by means of a hypodermic needle.

Inpatient. One who is admitted to a hospital or similar institution generally for temporary medical treatment and care.

Insomnia. A state of chronic sleeplessness.

Joint. Slang for marijuana cigarette. *See also* Marijuana.

Kindling. The strong reaction to cocaine that may include convulsions, seizures, or some form of psychotic behavior, and may be caused by changes in brain cells resulting from longtime cocaine use.

Laundering. Slang for moving illegal money through several banks or businesses so that it cannot be traced.

Lidocaine. A legal local anesthetic that may be substituted for cocaine in treatment.

Line. A term used to describe a row of cocaine powder, about 1 inch (2.5 cm) long and ⅛ inch (0.3 cm) wide, which users snort through a drinking straw or a rolled-up dollar bill.

Lithium. A chemical effective in treating depression and now believed to be able to block the euphoria produced by cocaine.

LSD. The popular name for lysergic acid diethylamide-25, one of the most potent mind-altering chemicals known.

Marijuana. The leafy, dried product of a cannabis plant that produces effects that have been described as a sense of well-being, dreamy relaxation, euphoria, and more vivid perceptions.

Narcotic. A drug that dulls a person's senses, relieves pain, and depresses or slows the nervous system.

Outpatient. One who lives in the community while receiving medical care from a hospital or clinic.

Overdose. The excessive consumption of a drug, causing symptoms ranging from stupor and agitation to coma and death.

Paranoia. A condition characterized by suspicious thinking and high levels of anger.

PCP. An abbreviation for phencyclidine, an illicit drug; also called angel dust. PCP use can cause hallucinations and violent or bizarre behavior.

Phencyclidine. See PCP.

Phoenix House. The nation's largest community system for drug-addiction treatment and rehabilitation.

Pot. Slang for marijuana. *See also* Marijuana.

Psychosis. A severe psychological reaction that may

result from prolonged cocaine use; characterized by hallucinations.

Replacement drug. A drug that is substituted in treatment for the one the patient has been abusing.

Residential treatment. A program in which the patient resides in the treatment facility, such as a hospital.

Rock. The street name on the West Coast for the form of cocaine known as crack.

Rocks. The small white, gray, or beige chunks or crystals of crack sold in clear plastic vials.

Runners. Smugglers who work for drug lords and have the job of getting illegal drugs into the United States or Canada.

Rush. The first onset of euphoria experienced by the drug user, said to be accompanied by a sense of strength, power, exhilaration, and the ability to succeed at any task.

Second-chance laws. The laws that allow courts to postpone sentencing for first-time offenders convicted of drug possession.

Sedatives. A group of drugs with calming or sleep-inducing effects.

Seizure. A condition in which the person becomes stiff and unmoving and loses consciousness.

Serotonin. A chemical in the brain believed to be responsible for sleep.

Snorting. Slang for inhaling a psychoactive drug such as cocaine.

Snow. Slang for cocaine.

Snowlight. Slang for the common reaction to cocaine use that makes objects appear fuzzy, with a halo around them.

Solvents. Chemicals that dissolve and remove impurities in substances.

Space base. A drug that combines crack and PCP.

Star speed. Another name for space base. *See also* space base.

Stimulants. A group of drugs that excite the central nervous system, producing euphoria, wakefulness, energy, and alertness.

Tolerance. A drop in response to a drug dose that occurs with continued use. The user needs stronger and stronger doses of the drug to get the same effect.

Trafficking. The obtaining, transporting, and selling of illicit drugs for commercial purposes.

Vasoconstrictor. A drug that closes up or tightens blood vessels.

Withdrawal. The process of stopping drug use and the unpleasant reactions it causes.

BIBLIOGRAPHY

Bureau of Justice Statistics
"Drugs, Crime, and the Justice System" A National Report of U.S. Dept. of Justice, December, 1992
Eighth District Report, Congressman James H. Scheuer, N.Y.,
"Drug Abuse: An Ever Growing Problem"
Eleventh District, Special Report from Senator Frank Padavan, N.Y.,
"Some Straight, Cold Facts on Crack"
National Clearinghouse for Alcohol and Drug Information
List of Publications, updated April 25, 1994
National Institute on Drug Abuse,
"Household Surveys"
"Cocaine Use in America," April 1986
"Cocaine: Pharmacology, Effects, and Treatment of Abuse," 1984
"Cocaine Use in America: Epidemiologic and Clinical Perspectives," 1985
"Treatment Research Report," 1985
"Drug and Alcohol Abuse: Implications for Treatment," 1983

"Public Health Issues and Drug Abuse Research," 1982
"Notes," No. 1 May 1986
Newsday,
"Hybrid Drug Combines Crack, PCP," August 9, 1986
"Cracks' Innocent Victims, the Babies," August 8, 1986
"Cars Confiscated in Crack Busts," August 5, 1986
Newsweek,
"Crack and Crime," June 16, 1986
"Cocaine Babies," July 28, 1986
"Hot Line on the Hot Seat," July 28, 1986
N.Y.S. Congress of Parents and Teachers,
"Cocaine," Spring 1986
N.Y.S. Division of Substance Abuse Services,
Update on Crack, February 1986
Report on Crack, May 1986
New York Times,
"At Schools, A Teach-in on Crack," October 1, 1986
"Use of Cocaine Seen Rising," September 29, 1986
"Drug Influx," September 26, 1986
"A 13-Year old Charged in Sale of Crack," September 18, 1986
"Crack as a Scapegoat," September 16, 1986
"Drug Crazed," September 12, 1986
"Battle over Crack," June 27, 1986
"Ending the Cocaine Habit," September 7, 1986
"Use of Crack: The Future," September 1, 1986
"Student Use of Cocaine Is Up," July 7, 1986
"From Colombia to Queens, Shadowy Route of Cocaine," July 24, 1986
"U.S. Troops to Aid Bolivians," July 15, 1986
"Bolivians Fear Drug War," July 31, 1986

"Examiner Confirms Cocaine Killed Bias," June 25, 1986
"Drugs Tied to Rogers' Death," June 29, 1986
"Cocaine's Vicious Spiral," August 17, 1986

Phoenix House News
Fall 1993, vol. 16, No. 3

San Francisco Chronicle,
"Drug Legalization Has Little Bay Area Support," October 1990

Time
"Crack," June 1, 1986
"Striking at the Source," July 28, 1986

FOR FURTHER READING

Buckalew, M. Walker. *Drugs & Stress.* New York: Rosen, 1993

Chatt, Andy. *Cocaine the Silent Killer, Self Help Manual.* Chatsworth, CA: Nocaine, 1991

Hawley, Richard A. *Thinking About Drugs & Society: Responding to an Epidemic.* New York: Walker, 1992

Kronenwetter, Michael. *Drugs in America.* New York: Simon & Schuster, 1993

Lee, Essie E. *Breaking the Connection: How Young People Achieve Drug Free Lives.* New York: Simon & Schuster, 1988

McCormick, Michele. *Designer-Drug Abuse.* New York: Watts, 1990

McMillan, Daniel. *Winning the Battle Against Drugs: Rehabilitation Programs* New York: Watts, 1991

FOR FURTHER INFORMATION OR HELP

COCAINE HELPLINE
1-800-662-HELP

NATIONAL COCAINE HOTLINE
1-800-COCAINE

NATIONAL CLEARINGHOUSE FOR DRUG ABUSE INFORMATION
P.O. Box 416
Kensington, MD 20795
301-443-6500

NATIONAL SELF-HELP CLEARINGHOUSE
33 West 42nd Street
New York, NY 10036
212-840-1259

PHOENIX HOUSE
164 West 74th Street
New York, NY 10023
212-595-5810

INDEX

Acupuncture, 109–10
Addiction to crack, 31, 33, 39, 106
Adrenaline, 36
AIDS, 30, 45
Air America, 63–64
Alcohol use, 33, 95, 109
Alexander, Pamela, 84
Angel dust, 59
Antidepressants, 108
Asset seizures, 85–86

Base houses, 60, 62
Berger, Dr., 86
Bias, Len, 7, 9, 14
Boarder babies, 96
Bolivia, 68, 70–72
Bonilla, Rodrigo Lara, 69
Borders, sealing of, 72–74, 76
Brain damage, 36
Bramble, Jim, 76, 78
Bremer, Lynn, 96
Britain, 88
Bromocriptine, 108–9

Bush, George, 72, 101
Byck, Robert, 23

Care and treatment, 92
  acupuncture, 109–10
  chemical treatments, 108–9
  compulsory treatment, 97, 99
  detoxification programs, 102–4
  drug-free living, 106
  federal policy on, 101
  hotlines, 26, 100–101, 110
  need for, 97, 99
  for professionals, 105
  psychological help, 103–5
  treatment on demand, 101, 110
Chemical treatments, 108–9
Child abuse charges for prenatal exposure, 95–97
Civil rights, 87, 89, 90, 92

125

Clinton, Bill, 101
Coca-Cola, 21
Cocaine
    addiction to, 39
    adulteration of, 51–52
    characteristics of users, 26, 28–29
    economics of, 86
    history of, 20–23
    increased use of, 11–12
    ingestion of, 52, 54
    laws on, 22
    manufacture and sale of, 48, 51–52, 68–69
    physical problems and, 28
    psychological problems and, 28
    reasons for using, 29
    smuggling of, 51, 73–74, 76
    values of, 20–22
    young people's views on, 12, 14
Cocaine Anonymous (CA), 106
Cocaine cartels, 68–69
Cocaine Helpline, 110
Coca plant, 20, 48
    worldwide production, 70
Colombia, 47, 48, 68–69
Compulsory treatment, 97, 99
Crack, 9
    addiction to, 31, 33, 39, 106
    body's absorption of, 35
    euphoria of, 35, 38
    first appearance, 19
    increased use of, 30–31
    name of, 19
    overdosing, 39–40
    physical effects, 35–37
    prenatal exposure, 40–42, 45
    psychological effects, 37–39
    smoking of, 17
    social effects, 44–46
    withdrawal, 42, 44, 105
    See also Manufacture and sale of crack; Users of crack
Crack houses, 16, 60
Crashing, 37, 38
Crime, 45

Decriminalization, 86–88
Demand reduction, 79, 81
    child abuse charges for prenatal exposure, 95–97
    compulsory treatment, 97, 99
    decriminalization, 86–88
    drug testing, 88–90, 92
    education programs, 92–93, 95
    laws against drug use, 81–82, 84–86, 93
    racial dimension, 82, 84
Detoxification programs, 102–4
Donahue, Terry, 11
Dopamine, 38, 108
Drug Enforcement Administration (DEA), 63–64
Drug-free living, 106
Drug paraphernalia, 84

126

Drug testing, 88–90, 92
Dysphoria, 38

Economics of cocaine, 86
Education programs, 92–93, 95
Euphoria of crack, 35, 38

Family therapy, 104
Freebase, 52, 54
Freud, Sigmund, 21

Gold, Mark S., 26, 28, 29, 30, 36, 39, 97
Gregg, David, 12

Hale, Clara, 42
Hallucinations, 37
Hardy, Kimberly Ann, 96
Heart failure, 36
Heroin, 35, 40
Hotlines, 26, 100–101, 110

Illanes, Fernando, 71, 72
Intensively supervised probation (ISP), 85
Intermediate sanctions, 85

Jackson, Jesse, 14
Johnson, Sterling, Jr., 19

Kindling, 40
Koller, Carl, 21

Langdon, Dan, 30
Laws against drug use, 22, 81–82, 84–86, 93
Lidocaine, 109
Lisi, Joe E., 19
Lithium, 108

Long, Terry, 12

Malnutrition, 36
Manufacture and sale of crack, 47–48
  brand names, 57
  children and, 62
  making crack from cocaine, 54, 57
  prices, 17, 29, 57
  space base, 59
  street selling, 60, 62, 79
  violence between sellers, 60
  See also Supply reduction
Mariani, Angelo, 21
Marijuana, 73
Mill, John Stuart, 99
Molloy, Dennis, 63
Money laundering, 76, 78
Montero, Doublas, 76

National Cocaine Hotline, 26, 110
Niemann, Albert, 20

Operation Blast Furnace, 70–72
Overdosing, 39–40

Paranoia, 37–38
Pawlowski, Joseph, 11
PCP (phencyclidine), 59
Pemberton, John Styth, 21
Peru, 68, 69
Prenatal exposure, 40–42, 45
  child abuse charges for, 95–97

Prohibition, 95
Pryor, Richard, 54
Psychological help, 103–5

Raskin, Mark, 30
Rawson, Richard, 105
Reagan, Ronald, 66, 72, 73
Rogers, Don, 9, 11
Rosecan, Jeffrey, 12

Santa Cruz Londono, José, 47–48
Sentencing guidelines, 81–82, 84
Serotonin, 39
Sexually transmitted diseases, 45–46
Shock incarceration, 85
Siegel, Ronald K., 20
Smialek, John, 9
Snowlight, 36
Social effects of crack use, 44–46
South Florida Task Force, 72–73, 76
Space base, 59
Strom, Lyle E., 82
Supply reduction, 63–64
    borders, sealing of, 72–74, 76
    crop substitution, 71–72
    disruptions in distribution, 76, 78
    military operations, 70–72
    public support for, 64, 66
    souce of drugs, focus on, 66, 68–72
Syphilis, 45, 46

Treatment on demand, 101, 110

United Nations Single Convention on Narcotic Drugs, 87–88
Users of crack, 15–16, 24, 26, 34, 102–4
    characteristics of, 29
    crack's appeal for, 29–30, 33
    first exposures, 31
    mood swings, 16
    social attitudes and, 33

Violence between sellers, 60

Wisotsky, Steven, 86, 87
Withdrawal, 42, 44, 105